DENISE AUSTIN'S
1-MINUTE
EXERCISES

DENISE AUSTIN'S 1-MINUTE EXERCISES

THE ONLY *PERSONAL TRAINER* YOU'LL EVER NEED

DENISE AUSTIN

PRODUCED BY

JEROME AGEL

PHOTOGRAPHS BY ANTHONY HOLMES

VINTAGE BOOKS
A DIVISION OF RANDOM HOUSE
NEW YORK

A Vintage Original, February 1987
First Edition

Library of Congress Cataloging in Publication Data
Austin, Denise.
   Denise Austin's 1-minute exercises.
   "A Vintage original."
   1. Exercise. 2. Physical fitness. I. Agel, Jerome. II. Title.
III. Title: 1-minute exercises. IV. Title: One-minute exercises.
GV481.A87   1987   613.7'1   86-40152
ISBN 0-394-74633-3

Manufactured in the United States of America
10 9 8 7 6 5 4 3 2 1

Designed by Beth Tondreau

Special thanks to Reebok International Ltd. for the shoes and activewear worn by
Denise Austin in this book and to Triangle Health and Fitness Systems for the mat
used in the exercises.

CONTENTS

Simple as these exercises may seem (and they really are), you always should consult with your doctor before embarking on any exercise program, especially if you have had surgery or physical problems, particularly with your knees, lower back, or neck.

DENISE AUSTIN'S
1-MINUTE
EXERCISES

INTRODUCTION

I want your body.

I want your heart—your fuel pump. I want your eight hundred muscles—your blood-oxygen-food motors. I want your head—your powerhouse.

I want *all of you* so that I can help you feel better, look better, play better, think better, work better—*be* better.

I need you for only a minute here and a minute there to help you shape up there, here, and everywhere. To help you work off tension and shuck fatigue and fat. To help you firm up the whole you.

I know what you are thinking:

"Come on, Denise, can *1-minute* exercises whenever I feel like doing them really do all that for me?"

No ands, ifs, or buts about it.

All exercise is preventive medicine. These commonsense, do-it-yourself, anywhere, anytime, no-sweat exercises are like getting extra interest on your savings. They work over your body from head to toe—neck, shoulders, arms, chest, back, waist, tummy, hips, thighs, buttocks, feet. They set off a chain reaction that revs up circulation, fights lassitude, stimulates a lifestyle that wards off and makes it easier to control health problems. The instantaneous benefit is release of tension.

Every survey confirms that few of us are really keeping ourselves in proper repair. We abuse our eyesight. We ride instead of walk. We sit around all day—and night. We take the elevator instead of climbing the stairs. We wolf down nutritionally poor fast foods and junk foods. We "recreate" with television sets, computer games, and VCRs. Before we know it, we are all sags, overhangs, and bulges. No wonder we feel blue. We may think about having a shapely shape, but if we're not fit, everything is too much work, too much bother, and the malady lingers on.

Fret no more. If you hate to exercise but recognize how necessary and effective it is, *these* exercises will get you moving. Moving is literally the first step. To be strong and limber, you must have active muscles—you must get 'em moving and keep 'em moving. Muscles were meant to be *used*. Underused, they deteriorate. They become flabby and weak. When they rest, they rust.

Unlike strenuous workout programs, these 1-minute exercises are for everybody and every body: children and teens and adults and grandparents. Do you know that one of the best-kept secrets in this country is the lack of youth fitness? George Allen, the chairman of the President's Council on Physical Fitness and Sports, was shocked to learn that "kids can't even run a mile as fast as someone in my shape can walk it," and he's in his sixties. Exercise is vital for proper growth and development. A day you don't work out is a day you can't ever make up. Fitness is not a fad.

You can do these exercises privately, in public, wherever you happen to be doing whatever you happen to be doing—at your desk, in your car, in the shower, in bed, on the phone, while walking. You don't have to go to a gym or to a health club. You don't have to change your clothes. (As I write this, I am also tucking my tummy.) You don't even have to get a sweat up. Which means no more excuses like "I don't look good in shorts" or "I don't have time" or "I hate to get all wet."

Headline: *Moderate Physical Exercise Significantly Increases Life Expectancy.* A continuing study of upwards of 20,000 Harvard alumni revealed that men who participated each week in activities that burned off 2000 calories or more had death rates one-quarter to one-third lower than those in the study who were less active. Men who walked merely 9 or more miles a week had a 21 percent lower risk of death than men who walked less than 3 miles a week. It turns out that inheritance of a sturdy constitution is less important to longevity than is continuation of adequate lifetime exercise.

News flash: *Overwhelming Evidence Shows Regular Exercise Helps Prevent Heart Disease, Osteoporosis, Diabetes, Depression, and Probably Other Ills as Well.*

I have been a physical fitness nut since I was a kid. It all started when I learned to skate on a pond in our backyard—I was four years old. When I was five, I couldn't wait to do cartwheels across the dance floor after a ballet class. At ten, I was trampolining away at the local Y. At eleven, I took gymnastic classes after school. At fourteen, I was enthusiastically putting in 5 hours a day, 7 days a week with a gymnastics team—practicing on the balance beam and the uneven parallel bars and doing vault and floor exercise. (Floor exercise was my favorite, because I couldn't fall off anything.) I had a choice of 21 college athletic scholarships. I majored in exercise physiology at the University of Arizona and was graduated from California State University, Long Beach, with a degree in physical education. I have taught aerobics classes and have trained hundreds of aerobics teachers. I started a business that set up fitness programs for corporations—healthier employees save corporations tons of money. (My booklet "Tone Up at the Terminals" describes exercises to help computer operators relieve eyestrain and weariness.) I have designed fitness programs for senior citizens and for teens. I have lectured and have demonstrated exercises in 45 states, and I have been telecast to all 50 and around the world as the fitness expert on the "Today" show. I have hosted my own television program, "Daybreak L.A.," and I have spread the gospel of physical fitness on hundreds of other programs. For more than five years, I have been involved with the President's Council on Physical Fitness and Sports. I have contributed hundreds of articles on fitness to national magazines and newspapers. And now I have my own daily television show —"Getting Fit with Denise Austin" on ESPN. I teach the mechanics of exercise, but I strive always to motivate and encourage everyone to enjoy the benefits that exercise affords. Can you tell that I love what I do?

As this little book quickly shows you how to be your own body expert—when, what, and how much to do—you'll become your own personal trainer. The 1-minute exercises will become part of your life. You'll start walking up stairs. You'll start stretching your hamstrings. You'll start toning your triceps—automatically, easily—while you're doing something else.

Once you've mastered the 1-minute exercises, you'll want to try the routines. I've included some longer ones for the more ambitious, and there's even a 10-minute sequence to do with a partner, which can be the most rewarding kind of exercise. You'll find a weekly workout schedule on the poster—my 7-Day Plan that takes only 20 minutes a day. And along the way I'll show you some important *do's* and *don'ts* to help protect you from injury as you make exercise a regular part of your day.

Yes, you can:

- wake in the morning feeling refreshed
- move with spring in your step
- have energy left at the end of the day
- have more zest for recreation
- sleep more soundly at night

You can do it all by saying *yes* to fitness opportunities. Get movin'!

TEST YOUR FITNESS

Self-assessment is the first step toward your goal—getting yourself into the shape you really want to be in.

The eight tests that follow measure strengths and weaknesses crucial to overall fitness. Take them now, then again every three months. You won't be measuring your fitness against that of others who differ from you in size, age, and body tone. Your only competitor is yourself. Keep a record of your progress—it will make you feel terrific as you go along. If you conscientiously do the exercises and routines I suggest, incorporating them into your lifestyle, genuine fitness will be inexorable and inevitable.

The tests are:

- Sit-and-Reach Flexibility
- Sit-Ups (to test abdominal strength)
- Push-Ups (to test upper-body strength)
- Balance
- Heart Rate
- Speed and Agility
- Power Jump (to test leg strength and power)
- Quick Body Fat

Note: Don't try any of the tests that you suspect will cause undue strain, and *stop* if you experience any pain. You can gain valuable information about your fitness without taking all eight. As with any physical activity, consult your physician before proceeding.

SIT-AND-REACH FLEXIBILITY TEST

A supple, flexible body is more fit for pleasure, sports, and work and is less injury prone. This test measures your flexibility, especially in the lower back and hamstrings. Flexibility comes with practice, so try this test as often as you feel like it. Record your inch-by-inch progress.

Place a strip of tape on the floor. Place a yardstick on the floor, perpendicular to the tape at the 14-inch mark, with the 1-inch mark toward your body.

Sit on the floor and extend your legs straight in front of you, straddling the yardstick. Place your heels on the floor about 5 inches apart, so that they just touch the near edge of the tape.

Keeping your legs straight, reach forward, with your hands side by side. Do not lead with one hand.

Touch the yardstick as far away as you can. Reach slowly and hold; don't bounce.

See how close you can come to touching your toes.

Record how far you stretch. If you reach past your heels, that's marvelous.

SIT-UP TEST

Abdominal strength is a key measure of overall fitness. Your abdomen is the core of your body and protects your vital organs and your back. (Lower back pain is one of the curses of middle age. Much of such pain is due to both a lack of flexibility and weak abdominal muscles.) This test is an excellent way to measure the strength of the abdominal muscles, because it only minimally uses hip, leg, and lower back muscles.

Place a strip of tape on the floor.

Lie on your back on the floor, with your knees bent and your feet flat on the floor on one side of the tape, your hips on the other.

Press your shoulders against the floor and extend your arms along your sides. Your fingertips should be about 3 inches from the tape. Place your palms flat on the floor.

Lift your head and shoulders off the floor in a partial sit-up, coming up only as far as necessary for your fingers to touch the tape.

Release.

Do as many of these sit-ups as you can in 60 seconds, counting each time your fingers touch the tape. Be sure that your shoulders touch the floor after each sit-up. If you can do more than 40 of these in 1 minute—*wow!*

This test measures upper-body strength—the strength in your chest, shoulders, and arms. Upper-body strength improves your appearance and posture and allows you to perform many tasks, especially those used in many sports, with greater ease.

N o t e : If you have high blood pressure, do not try this test.

Men: With your hands shoulder-width apart and your palms flat on the floor, fingers pointing forward, support yourself on your hands and the balls of your feet. Your shoulders, back, buttocks, and legs should form a straight line from head to heel.

Women: Rest your weight on your knees instead of on the balls of your feet, hands shoulder-width apart, with your lower legs bent up at a 90-degree angle. (Crossing your ankles will increase your stability.) Your body should form a straight, firm line from head to knee.

Bend your elbows, lowering your body until your chest all but touches the floor. Do not break the line of your body.

Raise yourself to the starting position, extending your arms fully.

See how many push-ups you can do in a minute. Record your results. If you can do 35—terrific!

BALANCE TEST

Good balance is essential for good posture and it enhances your ability in a variety of sports and tasks. Take this test to see how stable you are.

Stand on your right leg.

Place your hands on your hips.

Hook the top of your left foot just below your right calf muscle.

Raise your right heel off the floor.

Keep your balance as long as you can without moving the ball of your right foot or letting your right heel touch the floor (focusing your gaze several inches in front of you will help you concentrate).

Count the seconds between the time you raise your right heel and you lose your balance. Record the result.

Switch legs and repeat. Give yourself up to 6 trials per leg.

Try to balance yourself for an entire minute.

HEART RATE TEST

This test measures the fitness of your cardiorespiratory system—your heart and lungs. At rest, the average American's heart beats 72 to 80 times a minute. Fit people tend to have resting heart rates of between 50 and 65 beats a minute, because their hearts pump blood more efficiently. Their heart rates also return to normal more quickly after exercise.

N o t e : This test is physically taxing—if you become short of breath while climbing stairs, do not do it. And for some people, particularly those over 35, this test does not provide entirely accurate results. If you are in that age group, or are in any doubt about whether the test is appropriate for you, have your physician perform a maximal exercise stress test before you try this one.

Take your pulse: Place two fingers flat against the inside of your wrist (at the radial artery) or at the groove where the jaw meets the neck (the carotid artery). Count the beats for 10 seconds and multiply by six. Record your pulse.

Run in place or jump rope or climb stairs or march vigorously—or perform any other activity that keeps you moving continuously—for 3 minutes, to elevate your heart rate. (I like to put my favorite music on the stereo and run in place.)

Take your pulse again.

Relax. Do slow standing stretches for a full minute. (Make sure that your head does not drop below the level of your heart.)

Take your pulse a third time.

The quicker your heart rate returns to its pre-exercise rate, the fitter you are.

You can improve your cardiovascular fitness by engaging in aerobic activity for a minimum of 20 minutes at least 3 times a week. The activity should be vigorous enough to raise your heart rate to your "target heart rate zone," which is determined by the following formula: Subtract your age from 220 and multiply the result by .75. (If you are 40 years old, for example, your target heart rate is 220 minus 40, which is 180, times .75, or 135.) If your heart rate immediately after exercise exceeds that figure, you are working too hard and should slow down. If it is much below that figure, you are not working hard enough to exert a conditioning effect on your heart.

Check your cardiovascular fitness by doing this test at least once a month.

SPEED AND AGILITY TEST

This test measures such skills as coordination, reaction time, agility, and foot speed. While much of such ability is genetically determined, these skills can be improved with practice, making a host of activities easier.

N o t e : Do not do this test if you have knee or ankle problems.

Place on the floor a strip of tape 2 to 3 feet long.
Stand beside the line.
Keeping your legs together, jump from side to side back and forth over the tape, bending your knees as you land to absorb shock. Be sure you clear the line with each jump.
Jump as many times as you can for a full minute. Record the number of jumps.
If you can jump the line 100 times—fantastic.

POWER JUMP TEST

One definition of power is "the ability to release maximum force in the fastest possible time." The vertical jump is an exemplary test of power because it employs both leg power and arm power.

Grasp a piece of chalk in your right hand.

Stand with your right side to a wall, your heels together and planted on the floor.

Reach with your right arm as high as you can; make a chalk mark on the wall at that point.

Relax.

Jump straight up, as high as you can, extending your right arm straight overhead. Mark the wall at the peak of your jump.

Your score is the number of inches between the reach mark and the jump mark. For men, a 22-inch difference is an excellent score. For women, 12 inches or more is excellent. (Men usually jump higher than women.)

QUICK BODY FAT TEST

"For every inch the waistline exceeds the size of the chest, the pot-bellied person can deduct two years from how long he can expect to live."
                                        —Metropolitan Life Insurance Company bulletin

Excess body fat is recognized by the American Heart Association as a major factor in heart disease. Ideally, a man's waist should measure at least 5 inches less than his chest. A woman's waist should measure at least 5 inches less than her girth at a point just below the bustline. Here's my quick body fat test:

With the thumb and forefinger of one hand, pinch your tummy 2 inches to the side of your navel. There should not be more than ½ inch of fat between your thumb and forefinger. *Men* should also pinch the fat spots on the back of their middle upper arms and on their chest 2 inches above and outside the nipple. *Women* should also pinch the fat spots on the back of their middle upper arms and the backs of their thighs about 4 inches below the buttocks.

If you need to reduce body fat, you should not attempt to do so by restricting calorie intake alone, but by a proper balance between calories consumed and calories burned through exercise. Dieting alone slows your metabolism, making fat loss difficult and causing fatigue. Exercise speeds up metabolism and burns calories.

1-MINUTE
EXERCISES

Here we go.

The exercises are presented in a head-to-toe sequence to help you locate those that work the areas you want to concentrate on right away. The 1-Minute Saddlebag Slenderizer and the 1-Minute Hamstring Stretch, for example, are grouped together because they work the same area of the body. If you do 20 of these exercises in a day, you will have had a rewarding 20-minute workout by lights out.

1-MINUTE TAKE A DEEP BREATH

Marvin and Margaret Bush have been our closest friends since my husband and I moved to Washington, D.C., in 1983. They invited Jeff and me to join them and Marvin's parents at their summer home in Maine. We had a great time sunning, swimming, boating, socializing, and, of course, playing tennis. The Bushes are top-notch players, and so are the Austins (Jeff's sister is tennis star Tracy). While Jeff was playing with Marvin's dad, George Bush, I noticed that the Vice President took a deep breath just before he served. Undoubtedly, he deep-breathes all the time—while walking, while listening, while decision-making, while waiting. Deep breathing keeps the blood flowing, reduces stress, harnesses emotions, and maximizes performance.

Because breathing is automatic (10–16 breaths per minute), most people never give it a second thought, unless they fall into a lake. But most of us don't breathe fully enough to remove the toxins stagnating in the lower part of our lungs. The sage had it right: He who half-breathes, half-lives.

Taking deep breaths is a key to a fit body. Here's how:

Stand or sit.

Place your hands on your tummy.

Inhale slowly and deeply. Let your abdomen expand like a balloon. (Feel it with your hand.)

Exhale slowly, pulling in your tummy as you release stale air.

Keep repeating the sequence for 1 minute.

B e n e f i t : You'll become reacquainted with the breath you were born with.

"What are my chances when they load the bases with nobody out?" Dwight Gooden reflected. "I never doubt myself. I just step back, take a deep breath ..."

1-MINUTE FULL BODY STRETCH

I love to reach for the sky.

Sitting or standing, I raise my arms straight over my head and reach, reach, reach as high as I can. I hold my tummy in, stretch my rib cage, and try to pull down a cloud.

I then drop my arms to my sides.

I repeat the stretches for a full minute.

Benefits: Performed regularly with other stretches, helps your posture, makes you feel *terrif.*

1-MINUTE FACE GLOW

Many of us are living on the go-go-go. In my case, freneticism comes from hopping around the country and posing for photographers and doing live television interviews. My typical pace might include corporate pitches and dinner dates and a hundred phone calls and posting 50 letters. Your day might be a little different, but because we all have hectic times when we still must glow-glow-glow, I perfected a trick for looking alive and healthy on the spot. Here's how:

Standing or sitting, bend forward from the waist. (Bend your knees slightly if you're standing.)

Drop your arms and head toward the floor—let gravity get the hang of it for 30 seconds.

Tuck your chin into your chest.

Take a series of slow, deep breaths for 30 seconds.

Relax.

Tighten your stomach and raise your body to its upright position very slowly—one vertebra at a time.

You'll feel the glow coming on.

N o t e : Do not do this exercise if you have high blood pressure.

B e n e f i t s : Brings blood to the head, and therefore to the surface of your skin, rejuvenating you, switching on your beam.

1-MINUTE MINIFACIAL

Why do you think they're called "worry wrinkles"?

It's because wrinkles set in when you're thinking anxiously about a problem and your face becomes tense. It takes more muscles to frown than to smile. When your face is set in a worried expression, wrinkles start spreading like ripples on a pond. I've discovered a quick massage that gives your face a break from all of that.

Place your index fingers at the inside corners of your eyes, on either side of the bridge of your nose. Make small circles on your skin.

Keep making small circles as you work your index fingers all the way around your eyes.

Rub the bridge of your nose.

Work up and across your eyebrows.

Make 3 small circles over each temple.

Make small circles from the middle of your forehead out and up toward your hairline. Repeat twice.

Massage your cheeks and jaw with your thumbs and the pads of your fingertips—gently, gently.

Pinch up small sections of skin with light, quick motions, starting at the chin and moving up and out along the cheeks and jaw, for a count of 10.

Benefits: Releases tension, improves complexion by increasing circulation to your skin—*feels fantastic.* Let's face it: Who could ask for anything more?

1-MINUTE JAW RELAXER

Does your jaw feel tense most of the time? Do you grind your teeth when you sleep? Do you clench your jaw when you are under pressure? Do you get headaches at or near your temples, along with pain at the sides of your neck? If the symptoms sound familiar, you just might have Temporomandibular Joint Syndrome. (It's more commonly called T.M.J. Syndrome, and it afflicts tens of millions of Americans.) Check with your doctor or your dentist, especially if your jaw makes clicking, popping, or grating noises.

Some of us have habits that simply cause tension in the jaw. We clench a pencil between our lips or teeth, or cradle a telephone between neck and shoulder, or chew gum constantly, or bite our fingernails—all of which can cause excess tension in the jaw.

If you do suffer from T.M.J., treatment can be simple. All you may have to do is learn to relax your jaw whenever you are not eating or talking. My older sister, Kristine, is in dentistry in California. With her help, I developed this jaw relaxer. It's gotten terrific word of mouth. Kristine now teaches the exercise to her patients who suffer from T.M.J.

Close your lips, keeping your teeth apart.

Press the tip of your tongue against the roof of your mouth. Hold this position for 15 seconds.

Relax for 15 seconds.

Open your mouth as wide as possible.

Place three fingers—stacked vertically—between your teeth. (If your jaw muscles are so tight that three fingers won't fit, try two.) Hold for 15 seconds.

Relax for 15 seconds.

B e n e f i t s : If you do this exercise regularly, within a couple of weeks you'll notice reduced tension and pain in the jaw.

1-MINUTE VISION CARE

All of us get careless with our vision. We forget that our eyes are living tissue. Luckily, they don't wear out with ordinary use. But they do deserve the same kind of tender loving care we give our legs when we go for a run or our arms when we lift weights.

Good vision depends on adequate light. Most people spend an average of 12 to 16 hours a day under artificial light indoors. Often, we don't pay enough attention to whether we're seeing things in the right light. The next time you notice that your vision is blurring or your head is aching, don't run to the medicine cabinet for aspirin. Instead, take a look at the lamp you're using. Is it positioned correctly? Is it shedding enough light? In light that's bright enough for us to see clearly, the pupils of our eyes automatically become smaller in order to focus more efficiently on what they're seeing. When the light source is inadequate, pupils widen, causing strain and pain.

Avoid direct or reflected glare from the shiny surfaces of desks, tables, or floors. The areas where you work, read, and study should have overhead light distributed evenly throughout the room. If you work under flickering fluorescent bulbs, it's a good idea to have a lamp on your desk as well.

Remember to keep windows, bulbs, lampshades, and eyeglasses clean. Dirt can dim light and cause you to squint or strain your eyes.

Protect children from eyestrain. Make sure that the pages they read have large, clear type. As they become older and their eyes become stronger, they can begin to read the agate type of sports stats.

Eyestrain has become a particularly serious problem for the workers who use the more than 12 million desk-top computers already in this country. The typical computer clerk stares into the terminal about 6 hours each and every workday in a high-tech office. Just as your arms would become tired from holding a 20-pound weight for an hour, your eyes become fatigued by *staring hour after hour at that screen. 1-minute computer breaks should become the rule in the business world. And they work wonders for anyone who does close work. The idea is to relax your eyes by changing their point of focus periodically.*

Look away into the distance for 30 seconds.
Look at an even farther point for 30 seconds.

B e n e f i t : Alleviates eyestrain.

1-MINUTE VOICE-BODY CONNECTION

If you speak at public events, stay tuned.

Ed Hookstratten, the powerhouse agent who represents some of our top broadcasters, was the first to tell me about Lilyan Wilder, one of the best voice teachers in the country. The networks have all engaged her, and I have, too. Because I have to exercise and talk simultaneously during a lecture, it's vital that I experience the connection of voice and body. Lilyan showed me how. (This exercise, by the way, is also good for clearing the frog out of your throat when you wake in the morning with a squeaky voice.)

Stand up straight.

Bend your knees slightly.

Tip your torso forward from the hips. Let your head, neck, shoulders, and arms hang down like dead weight.

Swing your torso side to side—imagine you are an elephant swinging its trunk. Let your mouth hang open loosely.

Let your throat make whatever sounds come naturally as you sway. Don't be shy. Let the sounds burst forth—to get started, try singing a simple song like "Happy Birthday." Do what works best for you.

Sound off for a full minute, letting the words flow—they are triggered by the movement of the torso, so don't force them.

Benefits: Wakes you up vocally, links your voice with your body.

1-MINUTE ENERGY BOOSTER

Yes, once in a while I get pooped out.

Yes, once in a while I need to recharge my battery and get myself "up" for the next event.

After many a meeting, I've led my conferees through this energy booster. I remember a confab I had with David Wolper, the celebrated producer of the television series "Roots" and "North and South" and the opening ceremonies of the 1984 Olympics and the centennial celebration of the Statue of Liberty. He and two of his assistants and I, all in business suits, swung into this exercise in David's office in L.A.

When I visited the Soviet Union, in 1985, I led a grammar school math class in the booster—the kids lit up, I lit up.

Stand with your feet shoulder-width apart, your knees slightly bent.
Stretch your arms out to your sides, parallel to the floor.
Bend your elbows so that your fingers point toward the ceiling.
Extend your right arm straight overhead. Reach for the sky, extending up from your legs, stretching your whole right side. Hold for 10 seconds.
Release the stretch and return to starting position.
Stretch your left side.
Continue for a full minute, alternating sides.

Benefits: Gets the blood and oxygen pumping, stretches your upper body.

1-MINUTE ISOMETRICS

At the U.S. Open in 1985, I interviewed a number of the tennis stars for the "Today" show: Hana Mandlikova, Kathy Rinaldi, Mats Wilander, and others. I got to compare fitness notes with Martina Navratilova. My stomach is harder than Martina's, but her arms, especially her left arm—she's a southpaw—are stronger and harder than mine.

At Wimbledon, I once took advantage of a rainy day to get in some sightseeing. Which is how I came to see for myself that wondrous fact about those high-hatted guards at Buckingham Palace: They can indeed stand ramrod straight without (or so it appears) flicking a muscle or batting an eye, no matter how ingeniously someone tries to distract their attention. How in the world do they do it?

Here's their secret: Those men are concentrating one hundred and one percent on the isometrics they're executing. As part of their training, they learn to exercise this way while standing at attention. They imperceptibly work muscle against muscle from neck to toes to keep the blood pumping and to ward off boredom and fatigue.

The next time you're standing around—in a slow-as-molasses line in the post office, say—try this series that isolates specific muscle groups:

Stand tall and straight, derriere tucked in, knees bent slightly. Keep your shoulders back and down, your chest up.

Contract your hand muscles by making fists for a count of 10—and release.

Contract your forearm muscles by bending your wrists for a count of 10—and release.

Continue contracting and releasing—shoulders, chest, abdominals, back, buttocks, thighs, calves, feet. Contract each muscle group for a count of 10 —and release.

Benefits: Stimulates your body and your brain and maintains alertness, tones your muscles from head to toe.

1-MINUTE MINI-CHIN LIFT

Traveling salesmen tell me they have lots of idle time. They spend years behind the wheel and sitting in lounge cars and airplane cabins. And waiting for what seems an eternity in anterooms for the appointments in their appointed rounds.

Idle time can be turned into productive time. While you're stuck in traffic, you can give yourself a mini-chin lift.

Lift your chin just a bit—keeping your eyes on the road, of course. Raise your lower teeth over your upper lip, then lower them quickly. Repeat as many times as you can in 1 minute.

Benefit: A marvelous way to head off a double chin.

1-MINUTE NECK RELAXER

I put in 150,000 miles aloft every year. To ward off flying fatigue—poor circulation from all that sitting builds up kinks and tension in the neck—I've devised a neck relaxer that I can do in my seat. My seat companion, seeing what I'm doing, often joins me in this every-hour-on-the-half-hour exercise. (P.S. Drink one glass of water every hour you're in the air—it prevents dehydration.)

Sit up straight, with your shoulders relaxed, your neck extended nice and tall.

Lower your left ear slowly to your left shoulder. Hold for 15 seconds.

Roll your head to the right and hold your right ear to your right shoulder for 15 seconds.

Roll your head to the center. Touch your chin to your chest for 15 seconds. Keeping your chin to your chest, rock your head slowly to the left, then to the right. Semicircle continuously for 15 seconds. Be sure to keep your neck *long* throughout the entire exercise.

Relax.

N o t e : Never jerk your head or roll it backwards or in a full circle— such movements can compress the top two vertebrae and cause injury.

B e n e f i t s : Keeps your neck from getting stiff, relaxes a stiff neck and aching head.

1-MINUTE SHOULDER RELAXER

A few hours of inactivity can make your shoulders ache. Tension collects behind your neck and at the points your arms join the trunk of your body—you can feel like Atlas carrying the heavens on your shoulders. The best relief is an exercise that decreases muscle tension.

Lift your shoulders to your ears. Inhale. Lower your shoulders and exhale. Repeat.

Roll your shoulders up and back 5 times.

Roll your shoulders up and forward 5 times.

Execute 3 sets of shoulder rolls, backward and forward.

B e n e f i t s :   Releases tension and reduces stiffness in your neck and shoulders.

1-MINUTE SLOUCH STRETCH

Tom Brokaw, the urbane anchor of NBC's "Nightly News," assumes perfect posture when the camera's little red light goes on. He knows that perfect posture says a lot about a person. Body-language studies reveal that people who sit up straight project authority and confidence. This stretch will improve your posture and help you project such an image.

Clasp your fingers behind your neck.

Pull your elbows back as far as you can. Hold for 10 seconds.

Keeping your fingers clasped, try to bring your elbows together in front of you. Hold for 5 seconds.

Release your hands and relax for 5 seconds.

Repeat the sequence 3 times.

Benefits:
Keeps you from slouching, stretches your pecs, eases you into a positive posture.

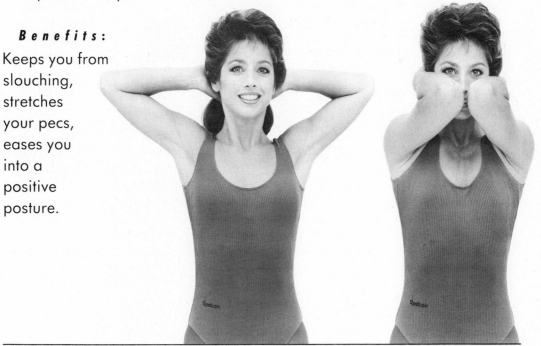

1-MINUTE MIDDLE-UPPER BACK STRETCH

Do you ever feel tight in your shoulders? Muscle fibers "adapt" physiologically to states of increased tension; in other words, a muscle will eventually stay in a state of unhealthy tension unless you do something about it.

To increase blood circulation and to ease tensed muscles, do what I do.

Put your right hand on your left shoulder.

Cup your right elbow with the palm of your left hand. Pull the elbow gently toward your left shoulder. Hold the stretch for 15 seconds, then release.

Switch sides and pull your left elbow toward your right shoulder.

Repeat.

Benefits: Stretches and relaxes the muscles between your shoulder blades.

1-MINUTE SEVENTH-INNING STRETCH

I have presented lecture-demonstrations to business groups coast to coast, from computer manufacturers to American Airlines. No matter what their ages or where they hail from, the audience's number-one question is always, "Denise, how can we beat off the 3 P.M. doldrums?"

My answer to everyone is my Seventh-Inning Stretch.

Stand up straight.

Place your hands on your shoulders.

Bring your elbows to the front of your chest and press them together. Feel the stretch across your upper back.

Draw your elbows back out to the sides and circle them up and back, exaggerating the motion. Circle for 30 seconds.

Relax.

Bring your elbows together in front of your chest again. Circle them down and forward for 30 seconds.

Relax.

Benefits: Loosens the muscles in your shoulders and upper back, gets you set to hit that bottom line again.

1-MINUTE CHEST DEVELOPER/BREAST LIFT

Although women's breast tissue is mostly fat, exercise can keep the underlying muscles strong and ward off droop, even with age. But weak chest muscles aren't a women-only problem. Sagging chest muscles contribute to bad posture in both sexes. So don't knuckle under to sags and droops. Fight gravity with this uplifting routine. Men should also sport a healthy chest.

Sit or stand with your knees slightly bent. Remove any finger rings or turn the stones inward.

Bring your knuckles together in front of your chest, keeping your elbows straight out to your sides.

Press your knuckles together for 10 seconds. Feel the chest muscles working.

Relax for 5 seconds.

Repeat the sequence 3 times.

B e n e f i t s : Firms and tones your pecs, promotes good posture.

1-MINUTE ARM STRENGTHENER

I'm on the professional tennis circuits a lot. It was at a tourney in La Quinta, near Palm Springs, that Jimmy Connors took me aside and showed me how he uses a tennis ball to strengthen his arms. This arm strengthener can be done anywhere—at a desk, in a car, at the movies, walking along the street—even in bed.

Grasp a tennis ball in the palm of your right hand.
Squeeze it as hard as you can for 30 seconds.
Release.
Grasp and squeeze the ball in your left hand for 30 seconds.
Release.
(You can extend this exercise by squeezing for 30 seconds, releasing, squeezing, releasing.)
Keep breathing while you squeeze —don't hold your breath.

Benefits: Tones and strengthens your forearms, biceps, hands, wrists— your whole arm.

1-MINUTE BRIEFCASE WORKOUT

Dr. Richard Keelor has been an inspiration to me since I met him soon after I was graduated from college, in 1979. At the time, he was director of programs for the President's Council on Physical Fitness and Sports. Today, he is president of LivingWell of America, a division of LivingWell, Inc., a Houston-based company that includes more than 400 health clubs across the nation. He's on the road a lot, but he never misses a chance for a quick workout. He showed me the exercise he loves to do while he's waiting for a plane. He uses his paper-loaded briefcase, instead of a weight or a barbell, to do arm curls.
(He's got great arms!)

Hold your briefcase at your right side with your right hand.

Pull your right elbow close to your body, with your palm facing forward.

Raise the briefcase slowly toward your chest, without moving your elbow.

Lower the briefcase to the starting position.

Raise and lower for a full minute.

Relax.

Switch arms and repeat.

Benefit: Strengthens your biceps.

1-MINUTE BACK-OF-THE-ARM STRETCH

My friend George Allen, the former professional football coach who is chairman of the President's Council on Physical Fitness and Sports, works out every day, rain or shine. He runs the mile from his home to a high school athletic field, where he runs around the quarter-mile track 8 to 12 times. He then runs home and heads straight for his garage, where he has a weight room. He lifts weights for about 40 minutes. Later in the day, when he's on the telephone, he lifts 10-pound dumbbells with his free hand.

George is always interested in learning a new exercise. After a meeting of the President's Council, I taught him this one:

Place your right hand in the middle of your shoulders behind your head. Give yourself a pat on the back.

Place your left hand on the right elbow. Push your right arm slowly down your back until you reach a point of tension. Feel a good stretch in your arm. (*Never stretch to the point of pain.*) Do not arch your back.

Hold the stretch for 30 seconds.

Release your arms. Relax.

Switch arms and repeat.

B e n e f i t :   Stretches the triceps and the latissimus dorsi.

1-MINUTE ARM FIRMER

Most of us don't work our triceps very much in normal daily activity, so the backs of our upper arms tend to get flabby. But triceps are important, both for appearance's sake and for your overall level of strength. I like to do this exercise as I'm working out on my stationary bicycle, to give my legs and arms—and heart—a workout at the same time. I turn on the news, to give my mind some exercise along with my body, and pedal away for 20 to 30 minutes, doing the underarm firmer most of the time. If my arms get sore, I rest them during the commercial breaks. (You should probably practice the firmer by itself for a few days before combining it with any other activity, though.)

Stand with your derriere tucked in and your back straight. Raise your arms toward the ceiling.

Bring your palms together and press as hard as you can.

Bend your elbows slowly, bringing your hands down toward your shoulder blades, continuing to press your palms together. Keep your elbows close to your head.

Raise your arms slowly.

Lower and raise your arms for a full minute, pressing all the while. Try to inhale deeply as you raise your arms. Try to exhale as you press your hands toward your shoulder blades.

Benefits: Firms and tones the backs of your arms.

1-MINUTE WRITER'S CRAMP RELIEVER

After hearing friends complain about "writer's cramp," I discovered it firsthand when I began writing magazine articles.

Writer's cramp is the tensing of muscles in the fingers and in the hand joints. It usually is caused by gripping the pencil or pen too tightly. Typists get cramps in their fingers and hands, too.

One day, a reporter for "USA Today," Sally Ann Stewart, told me about her problem with writer's cramp. I improvised an exercise that both relieves and prevents stress buildup in the hands. Ward off writer's cramp by doing this flex before you start typing or put pen to paper.

Stand or sit up straight.

Extend your right arm (or left, if you are left-handed) straight out in front of your body, palm up. With the opposite hand, grasp the fingers of the extended hand and bend them back as far as you can without causing pain. Hold for 15 seconds.

Release.

Turn the palm of your extended arm down, grasp the fingers with the opposite hand, and bend them toward the palm. Hold for 15 seconds.

Repeat.

Benefit: Releases tension in your hands, wrists, fingers, and forearms.

1-MINUTE PRESS-UPS

This one is a mite difficult, but it gets easier each time you do it. Try to do it once a day—it's good for the whole system.

Sit up straight in a chair or on a bench.

Place your hands on the armrests or beside your thighs on the seat. Lift your entire body, pressing with your arms to support yourself. Tighten your abdominal muscles. Keep yourself in a sitting position, with your knees bent, your back straight, your thighs parallel to the seat. You'll feel your abdominal muscles continue to contract.

Hold for 10 seconds. Exhale.

Lower your body and inhale. Relax for 5 seconds.

Repeat the exercise 3 or 4 times. Don't hold your breath!

Your goal is to lift your buttocks as high as possible. If your leg and abdominal muscles are extra strong, try to lift your body into a perfect L-shape, with your legs extended straight in front of you, perpendicular to your torso.

B e n e f i t s : Strengthens and tones your upper body—chest, arms, shoulders—and your quadriceps and abdominal muscles.

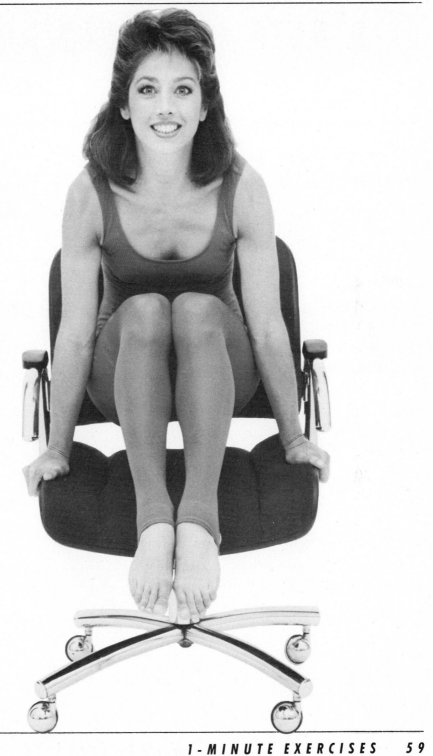

1-MINUTE AIR PUNCHING

It's been said that unless you're an orchestra leader or a house painter or a hanger of acoustic tiles, your arms never get enough exercise. Here's your chance to give your arms the break they need and work off aggression at the same time.

Punch the air in whatever manner feels most comfortable to you, alternating left and right punches. Pretend you're the heavyweight boxing champion of the world. (Just don't punch anyone out.)

Punch straight out in front of you.

Punch at the ceiling.

Punch down toward the floor.

Punch away for a full minute without pause, if possible.

Benefits: Increases circulation, helps firm jiggly arms.

1-MINUTE BEAUTIFUL BICEPS

I've been a friend of Lionel Richie and his wife, Brenda, for several years. When their dream house was built, complete with exercise equipment, I showed Lionel a progressive weight routine to tone, firm, and build up his muscles. But when he's on tour, he can't go to gymnasiums to work out, because his presence would create too much hoopla. So I taught him a three-way push-up that he can do in his hotel suite. The exercise keeps his biceps toned and gorgeous and it pumps him up so that he can go "All Night Long." You'll find you can even do this exercise at work.

Assume a push-up position, with your hands shoulder-width apart, palms flat on the floor, fingers facing forward. (*Men:* Support yourself on your hands and the balls of your feet; your body should form a straight, firm line from head to toe. *Women:* Support yourself on your hands and knees, so that your body forms a straight, firm line from head to knee; you may find it more comfortable to cross your ankles behind your knees.)

Lower your body slowly, almost to the floor, bending your elbows. Be sure to keep your back straight, your body aligned.

Raise your body slowly, straightening your arms.

Do as many push-ups as you can in 20 seconds.

Turn your hands so that your fingers are facing in and your elbows point away from your body. Do as many push-ups as you can in 20 seconds.

Turn your hands so that your fingers point outward. Do as many push-ups as you can in 20 seconds. (This position is the most difficult of the three.)

B e n e f i t s : Strengthens your arms, shoulders, and chest; a good way to break up a frenzied schedule.

1-MINUTE CRAB WALK

Kids are the best toys ever made, my writing colleague Jerry Agel says. They never stop moving, their batteries never run down. Have you tried keeping up with a kid lately?

Playing with kids rejuvenates adults. The next time you're on the floor with a child at least three years old, teach him or her to do the Crab Walk.

Squat on your heels.

Place your hands on the floor behind you, with your fingertips facing your buttocks. Raise your buttocks at least 12 inches off the floor.

Crab walk forward on your hands and heels for 5 steps—right hand advances with left foot, left hand advances with right foot.

Crab walk backward for 5 steps.

Crab walk forward and backward for a full minute.

B e n e f i t s : Strengthens your upper body, arms, and thighs, dispels crabbiness.

1-MINUTE ACROSS-THE-CHEST TOWEL STRETCH

This easy exercise leads to automatic good posture; everyone else will sit up and take notice. I like to do it just before hopping into the shower.

Stand with your back straight, feet shoulder-width apart, knees slightly bent, arms at your sides.

Grasp the ends of a bath towel held lengthwise and stretched taut. Raise it over your head.

Press your arms back slowly until you reach a point of tension. Hold for 30 seconds. Keep your back straight (don't arch) and your abdominal muscles contracted, and remember to breathe. Squeeze your buttocks. Let your arms and shoulders—not your lower back—do the work.

Release.

Repeat the sequence.

Benefits: Stretches your torso and shoulders, increases flexibility, improves posture.

1-MINUTE WAKE UP YOUR SPINE

Quick! Try to think of someone you know who has great posture. Most of us probably can't name more than two or three people. Most people have poor posture because they don't exercise enough. Poor posture leads to tired spines that are begging for relief.

Here's an excellent stretch that will wake up your spine. It's particularly effective immediately after awakening. It gets your circulation going after a full night's sleep and—if you sleep on your stomach, especially— stretches out your vertebrae.

Lie on your back with your legs extended straight out in front of you.

S-t-r-e-t-c-h your whole body. Imagine that you are making yourself taller. Hold for 10 seconds.

Relax for 10 seconds.

Bend and stretch your torso to the right, extending your arms and shoulders and keeping your legs and hips straight and still. Feel the stretch in your sides. Hold for 10 seconds.

Relax for 10 seconds.

Bend and stretch your torso to the left, extending your arms and shoulders. Hold for 10 seconds.

Release for 10 seconds.

Benefits:
Stretches your whole body, especially your spine; revs you up for the day.

1-MINUTE YOGA RELAXER

When I was in Alma-Ata in the Soviet Union, about 100 miles from the Chinese border, I led my group (I was part of the Delegation for Friendship Among Women) on a walk every morning. We'd wind through the park across the street from the hotel and pause to watch about 15 elderly men and women exercise. They did this yoga relaxer, which feels so good you'll want to do it again right away. It's as though you're realigning your back and putting every muscle into its proper place. You don't have to do it in a park, of course. You can do it in your living room while watching television, for example—instead of going to the fridge when a commercial comes on, do this stretch until the program resumes.

Kneel on the floor with your feet tucked under your buttocks, your palms on the floor beside you.

Slide your arms forward slowly, reaching out along the floor as far as you can. Lower your head between your arms.

Breathe slowly and rhythmically—inhale to a count of 5, exhale to a count of 5. Hold the stretch for a full minute, continuing to breathe slowly.

Release.

Note: Do not do this exercise if you have knee problems.

Benefit: Eases tension in your lower back.

1-MINUTE SPINAL STRETCH

Raking leaves, hoeing the flower beds, picking vegetables, and cutting the grass can take a toll on the spine if it's not properly limbered up first. Willard Scott, the "Today" show's witty weatherman, is a gardener, not to mention my great and good friend. He and his family have a 25-acre farm in northern Virginia, and Willard loves to exercise his green thumb. One Sunday evening, when we were flying out together on the Eastern shuttle to do "Today" in New York the next morning, Willard mentioned that the muscles in his back were sore. While we were waiting for our driver at LaGuardia, I showed him an exercise to do both before and after yardwork.

Stand with your feet about 12 inches apart and your knees slightly bent. Clasp your hands behind your back, over your buttocks.

Raise your hands back and up, as high as you can.

Lean back slightly, without arching your back, and push your pelvis forward a bit, keeping your knees bent. Lift your sternum and relax your neck. Contract your abdominals and squeeze your buttock muscles.

Hold for 15 seconds.

Bend forward slowly from the waist, until your upper body is perpendicular to your legs—or as nearly so as possible.

Again pull your arms gently up and back, keeping your hands clasped. Tuck your chin to your chest. You'll feel a good stretch through your spine and—if you really stretch—in your legs and arms.

Hold for 15 seconds.

Roll up slowly to your starting position, one vertebra at a time.

Repeat the entire sequence. Remember to breathe normally throughout.

Note : Do not do this exercise if you are prone to lower back pain.

Benefits : Stretches your spine, increases flexibility, wards off soreness.

1-MINUTE BATH STRETCH

Whether your body is morning sleep-steeped or evening stressed-up, there may be no better prescription than a bath. Lolling in a tub of water can nudge your body toward waking or toward unwinding. Be careful, though—bathwater that's too warm can lull you to sleep! Bubble bath is a luxurious pick-me-up, bath oil smoothes dry skin, and a shake of mineral salts soothes muscles aching from a workout.

I begin relaxing the moment I feel the warm water play on my body. I take advantage of the water's muscle-soothing power by going into my glorious stretch for spine and legs.

Sit up straight in bathwater to your waist, with your legs stretched out in front of you and your feet together.

Inhale.

Round your back and gently lower your head toward your chest. Exhale slowly. (Don't dunk your head!)

Hold for 20 seconds.

Straighten your back, uncurling one vertebra at a time until you're upright again. Inhale.

Again gently lower your head to your chest, but this time reach for your toes with your fingers. Rest your hands on your legs if you can't reach your toes. Feel the stretch in your spine and legs. Hold for 20 seconds.

Exhale slowly.

Straighten your spine, uncurling one vertebra at a time, until you're upright again.

Repeat the sequence.

B e n e f i t s : Stretches tired back and leg muscles, relaxes you.

TOE TOUCHES DO'S AND DON'TS

DON'T try to bend over from a standing position to touch your toes—this familiar (but hazardous) stretch places too much pressure on the lower spine. Bouncing increases the possibility of injury.

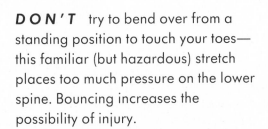

DO sit on the floor, with your legs extended in front of you and your knees slightly bent. Stretch gently, reaching forward toward your toes (don't worry if you can't touch them), and hold; don't bounce.

1-MINUTE WINDMILL

Is there anyone who doesn't want to trim his or her hips and waistline? The 1-Minute Windmill does it in a breeze. I've always wanted to have a company's entire typing pool do this one together—on a warmish day, it'd cool off the pool.

Sit in a chair with your feet on the floor, about 24 inches apart.

Bend forward from the hips and try to touch your right hand to your left foot. Extend your left arm back and up well above your head. Hold for 5 seconds.

Switch sides and repeat.

Repeat the sequence 5 times, alternating sides.

Benefits: Helps trim your hips and waistline, stretches your back.

1-MINUTE KNEE KISS

Loreto, on the east coast of Baja California in Mexico and surrounded by vast desert, is the improbable home of a spectacular five-star tennis resort that hosts an annual festival with John McEnroe as the headliner. When my husband organized the festival a couple of years ago, I went along to pick up some tennis pointers from Hana Mandlikova, Kathy Rinaldi, Steffi Graf, and Melissa Gurney. One morning, I led everyone, including hundreds of visitors, through an aerobics class on center court. We had a ball.

Loreto's stadium is architecturally creative, but, as in most stadiums, the seats are hard and without back support. While watching a titanic match between Hana and Steffi, I became aware that my back was pooping out on me. The tennis was first-rate, so I wasn't about to leave. Fortunately, I know how to relieve the pressure on a tired back, even while sitting down.

While seated, pull your right knee in to your chest with both hands and plant a kiss on it. Hold for 10 seconds.

Release.

Switch legs and repeat.

Repeat the sequence 3 times.

Benefits: Relieves lower back pain, stretches your lower back muscles.

1-MINUTE ABDOMINAL CURL

Lie on your back, with your knees bent and the soles of your feet flat on the floor or mat.

Fold your arms over your chest.

Curl up slowly, until your shoulder blades are just clear of the floor or mat. Keep the small of your back flat against the floor or mat and your abdominal muscles tight. Relax your head and neck. Hold for 5 seconds.

Slowly lower yourself back down, one vertebra at a time.

Repeat the sequence 10 times.

B e n e f i t :   Strengthens your upper abdominal muscles.

SIT-UPS DO'S
AND DON'TS

DON'T do traditional straight-leg sit-ups—they are less effective than many other exercises in strengthening the abdominal muscles. More important, they put a severe strain on the spine, which can lead to injury and chronic back pain.

DO bend your knees to protect your back. Curl up only half way, keeping your eyes on the ceiling. Better yet—try some of my 1-minute exercises for the abdominals!

1-MINUTE STUNNING STOMACH

A big belly isn't something you should stomach, especially when you can have a tummy as trim and tight as you've imagined. Try these exercises, back to back or just the one you're most comfortable with.

Lie on your back, with your legs fully extended.

Pull your right knee in to your chest, grasping it just below the knee with both hands. (If you have had knee problems, you may prefer to grasp *behind* the knee.)

Lift your head and shoulders off the floor. Keep your eyes on the ceiling.

Lift your left leg slightly off the floor and keep it straight. Keep your lower back pressed against the floor.

Hold for 10 seconds.

Release.

Switch legs and repeat.

Repeat the sequence 3 times, alternating legs.

Benefits: Tones the rectus abdominis and the front of the thigh, stretches the back.

Lie on your back, with both knees bent and your feet flat on the floor.

Place your fingertips behind your ears.

Bring your right knee in to your chest and touch your left elbow to it.

Release.

Bring your left knee in to your chest and touch your right elbow to it.

Release.

Repeat as many times as you can for a full minute, alternating knees and elbows.

Benefits: Strengthens and tones your abdominal muscles.

Get down on all fours.
Take a deep breath.
Exhale and curve your spine up toward the ceiling, pulling in your stomach. Let your head hang down. Hold for 5 seconds.

Inhale and arch your back, keeping your stomach muscles taut. Look up.
Hold for 5 seconds.
Relax.
Repeat the sequence 3 times.

Benefits: Strengthens and relaxes your back muscles, tones your abdomen.

Note: If you have had neck or shoulder problems, you will probably prefer the third exercise to the first two.

1-MINUTE TUMMY TUCK

The day after Jeff and I were married four years ago, we flew from Los Angeles to Venice. It was a half-day flight, and Jeff didn't know what he was in for. People have said that sitting next to me on a long flight is better than watching the movie.

I do one minute of tummy tucks every hour I'm in the air. My honey was a little startled at first, but by the sixth hour he gave it a try, too. He got the knack right away, and now he really likes our airborne workouts—he even tummy tucks at his desk. The 1-Minute Tummy Tuck is easy. Once you get into it, you'll have the confidence to invite your seatmate to join in the fun. (In case you're wondering, we had a glorious honeymoon in Italy. And yes, I tummy tucked in a gondola at the stroke of midnight.)

Sit up straight.

Firmly grasp the armrests or the edge of your seat to stabilize your body. Be careful not to hunch your shoulders.

Raise both knees toward your chest, keeping your legs together.

Bow your head and shoulders slowly toward your knees, and tuck your tummy underneath. (You'll know you're doing the exercise correctly when you feel as though your navel is pressing toward your spine.)

Hold the tucked position for 10 seconds.

Release. Return to an upright sitting position.

Repeat 5 times.

You may find this a bit awkward at first, and it may take you a little longer than 10 seconds to do each tummy tuck properly. Practice makes perfect. Try it right now.

Benefits: Tones and tightens your abdominal muscles, stretches your neck and back.

1-MINUTE ADVANCED SIT-UP

"Come on, Denise, give us a hard one."

When I'm asked by a class to give 'em a real test, I introduce this one—but only if the exercisers are in good shape to begin with.

Lie on your back with your legs elevated until they are perpendicular to the floor, arms extended behind your head. (You may prefer to prop your legs against a wall for balance.)

Slowly raise your arms, shoulders, and head toward your toes, as high as you can go without raising your lower back from the floor. Keep your stomach tight and tucked in

Hold for 10 seconds.

Release.

Repeat up to 5 times.

Benefits: Tones and strengthens your whole abdominal area.

1-MINUTE TORSO/BACK STRETCH

Lie on your back on the carpet or mat.

Bend your knees and keep them together. Extend your arms straight out to the sides.

Pull your knees in to your chest. Roll them together to the floor on your right. Hold for 10 seconds.

Roll your knees back across your body to the floor on your left. Be sure that your shoulders stay flat and your stomach stays tucked. Hold for 10 seconds.

Repeat 2 times.

B e n e f i t s : Stretches and relaxes your lower back and torso.

1-MINUTE HIP STRETCH

Hips are on everybody's toughest-to-tackle list. They just don't come in standard shapes and sizes—they're curvy or long or narrow or wide or full. But no matter what kind of hips you have, you'll say "hip-hip-hooray" for this muscle shaper.

Bend both knees and sit cross-legged on the floor with your right foot on top of your left knee. Keep your back straight.

Extend your hands side by side in front of you.

Bend forward from the hips until you feel a stretch in the hips, buttocks, and lower back.

Hold and deepen the stretch for 30 seconds.

Release and repeat.

B e n e f i t s : Elongates your spine, improves flexibility in your hips.

1-MINUTE HIP FLEXER

Colleen Keegan is a very dear friend of mine. She's an executive producer with MTV, and she produced my videos "Rock Aerobics" and "Rock Hard Tummies." Colleen lives in New York City and is constantly attending this fancy party or that prestigious social affair or dinner. Her clothes are (as she says) "to die for" and usually form-fitting. She wants always to look "terrif" in them, so I suggested the following easy exercise to help keep the sides of her waist and her hips slim, slim, slim.

Stand with your right side about a foot and a half from a wall.

Place your right hand on the wall at about shoulder height, with the fingertips pointing up and the elbow bent.

Without moving your feet, try to touch your hip to the wall. Keep your shoulders aligned with your feet. Hold for 15 seconds.

Return to the starting position. Relax.

Repeat.

Turn and repeat the exercise on the left side.

Benefits: Tightens and stretches your waist and hip muscles.

1-MINUTE EXERCISES TO SHRINK MIDDLE-AGE SPREAD

As time zips by, many women acquire a fleshy bra overhang, which can make it embarrassing to wear bare-backed dresses. Men's fat deposits, on the other hand, are mostly in the spare tire (the Pillsbury Doughboy tummy) and in the love handles (the fatty areas around the hips). Here are ways to get rid of both kinds of midriff bulge.

Stand with your knees bent.

Extend your arms out to the sides, with your elbows bent so that your forearms are parallel to the floor.

Twist from the waist from left to right, punching from side to side as you twist. To allow yourself maximum reach and movement, lift the heel of your right foot as you twist to the left, and the heel of your left foot as you twist to the right.

Twist and punch for a full minute.

Benefits: Works and tones your torso and upper back.

Stand with your feet shoulder-width apart, pointing outward, and your knees bent as in a *plié* position.

Place your fingertips behind your ears and extend your elbows out to the sides.

Bend to the right from the waist, bringing your right elbow as close to your right knee as you can. Keep your back straight and bend directly to the side—don't hunch forward.

Return to an upright position.

Bend to the left.

Continue bending from side to side, as often as you can, for a full minute.

N o t e : Do not do this exercise if you have lower back pain or knee problems.

B e n e f i t s : Tones the sides of your waist, trims love handles.

TRUNK TWISTS *DO'S* AND *DON'TS*

DON'T twist rapidly—too-rapid movement can result in back injury or pulled muscles.

DO twist slowly, to give the muscles along the sides of the waist and trunk a good stretch. Hold your arms horizontal and in a straight line with your shoulders and keep your hips forward.

1-MINUTE SIDE STRETCH

Sit up straight.

Interlace your fingers and raise your arms straight over your head, palms down.

Press your arms backward as far as you can without straining. Don't bend your elbows.

Slowly bend to the left from the waist. Feel the stretch all the way down the side. Hold for 5 seconds.

Return to an upright position, then slowly bend to the right. Hold for 5 seconds.

Continue bending to the left and to the right, holding each stretch, for a full minute.

Benefits: Stretches and strengthens the muscles along the sides of your body from shoulders to hips.

1-MINUTE WAIST TWIST

Most of us spend an awful lot of time in automobiles. I've heard of people who won't walk even half a block for a quart of milk. And even when we're not being lazy, a lot of us end up spending hours waiting around in parked cars for one reason or another.

The next time you're sitting in a parked car, turn waiting time into trim-your-waistline time.

Sit comfortably, with your back straight.

Twist your torso toward the right, far enough that you can grab the back of the seat with both hands. Feel the stretch through your waistline, upper arm, and back.

Hold for 15 seconds.

Release.

Twist toward the left.

Repeat the stretch on each side. If you want to work a little harder—or have longer to wait—try holding the stretch for 20 seconds.

Benefits: Works and stretches the muscles on your sides—the internal and external obliques.

1-MINUTE PELVIC TILT

Lie on your back, with your knees bent and your feet flat on the floor, shoulder-width apart.

Extend your arms along your sides.

Tighten your abdominals and squeeze your buttocks muscles as tightly as possible, tilting your pelvis up and rounding and pressing your lower back against the floor.

Hold for 10 seconds.

Lower your pelvis to the floor.

Repeat 4 times.

Benefits: Strengthens your lower back and abdomen, reduces back strain.

1-MINUTE BUTTOCKS STRETCH

Get down on all fours.

Slide your left leg straight back. Tuck your right heel under your left hipbone.

Press your left buttock toward your right heel. Lower your elbows to the floor. Concentrate on relaxing. Feel the stretch in your right buttock and outer thigh.

Hold the stretch for 30 seconds.

Return to all fours. Do the stretch on the other side.

Note: Skip this exercise if you have back, hip, or knee problems.

Benefits: Stretches your gluteus maximus and the muscles in your hips and outer thighs.

1-MINUTE WALL SIT

Anyone who knows me knows I talk on the telephone a lot. My business depends on the phone. I'm really very busy, rushing here, flying there, so the phone has become the best way to keep up with my friends and to check on the progress of my professional activities.

But, as you might guess, I never, never just sit there when I'm on the phone. It'd be a waste of perfectly good exercise time.

Lean back lightly against a wall. Flatten your spine against the wall.

Lower your body along the wall until your knees are bent to at least a 45-degree (and no more than a 90-degree) angle. Pretend you are sitting in a chair.

Hold for as long as you can, up to 60 seconds.

B e n e f i t s : Tones and strengthens your quadriceps; especially great for skiers.

KNEE BENDS *DO'S* AND *DON'TS*

DON'T bend your knees all the way to a 90-degree angle; the strain on your knees can damage cartilage and injure your patella, resulting in permanent damage and chronic knee problems.

DO bend your knees only about halfway (to a 45-degree angle approximately—less if you experience undue strain or have knee problems).

1-MINUTE WINTER WARM-UP

Outdoor activities can be a ball in the winter, but you need to make sure you're dressed warmly enough for them. Wearing layers of clothing—including a thick wool sweater and heavy trousers—should keep you warm for skating, skiing, or running. Down-filled gloves and wool socks will help protect your hands and feet. And a woolen hat is a must, because at least 40 percent of your body heat can be lost through a bare head.

When you're all dressed and ready to go, this cross-country lunge will get your blood moving.

Stand tall.

Take a giant step forward with your right foot.

Bend your right knee until it forms a perfect right angle (no further, or you will put too much stress on the knee). Your knee should be directly over—not in front of—your ankle.

Place your hands on the floor on each side of your right foot.

Lower your hips without changing the position of either leg. Keep your left leg as straight as possible.

Hold the stretch for 30 seconds.

Release. Stand up straight.

Repeat the stretch with the left leg forward.

Benefits: Stretches your hips and groin, increases flexibility, helps you achieve your full range of motion.

1-MINUTE AQUACISES

My friend Casey Conrad, a former executive director of the President's Council on Physical Fitness and Sports, introduced me to these aquacises. His Aqua Dynamics program promotes bobbing as "a particularly good conditioning activity in water. You make a feet-first surface dive, then push your head and shoulders out of the water—you bob much as a cork held under water bobs when released. . . . Bobbing forces the breathing, which itself is an exercise; quick inhaling and forced exhaling require greater effort, and the swimmer benefits that much more from the aquacise." So when you find yourself near a pool—assuming you can swim—plunge into these aquacises.

Walking Twists
Stand in waist- to chest-deep water with your feet slightly apart.
Lace your fingers behind your neck and put your elbows out to the sides.
Raise your left knee and touch it with your right elbow. (Yes, you may bend a bit.)
Return to starting position.
Raise your right knee and touch it with your left elbow.
Return to starting position.
Continue alternating knees and elbows for 30 seconds.

Leg Scissors

Stand in the water and hold on to the gutter or edge of the pool. Extend your body out fully behind you.

Push your legs out to the sides in a wide "V" position.

Bring your legs together. Cross your left leg over your right leg.

Uncross your legs. Open them wide again.

Bring them together, then cross your right leg over your left leg.

Uncross your legs.

Continue opening, closing, and crossing your legs for 30 seconds.

B e n e f i t s : Tones and firms your legs, especially your inner and outer thighs.

1-MINUTE SADDLEBAG SLENDERIZER

Even if you're slender everywhere else, those curves in the outer thighs can collect fat. Fortunately, those "saddlebags" can be unpacked.

One of the best ways of trimming them is the side leg lift. You can do it standing just about anyplace—behind a counter, at a desk, while pumping gas, waiting in a grocery check-out line, diapering the baby.

Stand straight and tall. Rest one or both hands on a sturdy object for support.

Keeping your hips stationary, raise your right leg directly to the side, foot flexed. Lift yourself as high as you can.

Lower your leg.

Lift 20 times in 30 seconds.

Repeat with your left leg.

B e n e f i t s : Trims your outer thighs, gives you a sleeker look; strengthens the hip abductors.

1-MINUTE REAR LIFT

Many women complain that their bodies are pear-shaped. That's because women tend to store fat in their buttocks and upper legs.

You can give your derriere a pick-me-up even while you're cooking or ironing or loading the dishwasher or waiting in line at the ski lift.

Stand straight.

Lift your right leg straight out behind you—only a couple of inches off the floor. Point your toes.

Squeeze your buttocks tight—feel the muscles tense and work. Keep your hips facing straight ahead; don't slouch.

Return your foot to the floor.

Lift and squeeze and lower 20 times.

Relax.

Switch legs and repeat.

B e n e f i t s : Tones and tightens the backs of your thighs and your buttocks.

1-MINUTE HAMSTRING STRETCH

I've been known to do this stretch in the darndest places. I've stretched my legs parallel to the floor of airliners. I've propped my feet—one at a time, of course—on the bathroom sink while drying my hair. I've even plopped them on the kitchen counter while preparing dinner with my husband.

Wherever you do it, it's a great way to loosen your hamstrings and prevent a host of problems. (Tight hamstrings can pull on the muscles of the pelvis, which in turn pull on the back muscles, causing discomfort and injury.)

Stand straight in front of a stable, waist-high fixture, such as a table.

Raise your right heel slowly and brace it on the edge. Keep both legs as straight as possible.

Lower your nose as close as possible to your right knee or shinbone, sliding your arms along your leg until you reach a point of tension, keeping your back flat. (Don't push yourself farther than you can stretch comfortably.)

Hold for 30 seconds. Don't bounce—bouncing can strain or tear muscles. Breathe deeply; don't hold your breath.

Return to an upright position. Lower your leg.

Repeat the stretch with your left leg.

Variation: Lie on your back on a carpet or mat, with your knees bent and your feet planted on the floor.

Raise your right leg and grasp it with both hands.

Straighten your right leg and pull it toward your chest. Keep the small of your back pressed against the floor.

Hold for 15 seconds.

Release.

Switch and stretch the left leg.
Repeat the stretch on both sides.

Benefits: Increases the flexibility of your hamstrings, helps prevent back pain, re-energizes your legs.

HURDLER'S STRETCH *DO'S* AND *DON'TS*

DON'T bend your lower leg back behind you—it puts undue strain on the knee joint and stresses the ligaments, which can lead to chronic knee problems and injury.

DO bend the knee to the front, tucking your lower leg in toward the opposite thigh. Stretch gently toward the straight leg, without bouncing.

1-MINUTE QUADRICEPS STRETCH

You have about 800 muscles in your body. The quadriceps—the four muscles in the front of your thighs—are among the largest and strongest. They are used in walking, biking, climbing, and so on. Because they are vital to most actions, it is essential to keep them flexible. You need to stretch them to relax them. Jay Schroeder, the Washington Redskins' heralded young quarterback, told me that the 1-Minute Quadriceps Stretch is one of the exercises that athletes perform most often.

Stand straight. Place your right hand on a stationary object for balance.

Bend your left leg up behind you, keeping your right leg straight and your knees together. Grasp your left leg by the ankle with your left hand and pull up. Stand straight— don't bend at the waist. Feel the stretch in your left thigh.

Hold the stretch for 10 seconds.
Release.
Repeat twice.
Switch sides and stretch your right leg.

Variation: Lie on your stomach with your arms extended straight in front of you.

Bend your right leg up behind you and grasp the ankle with your right hand. Try to touch your heels to your buttocks.

Hold for 30 seconds.

Release.

Switch legs and repeat.

Benefits: Stretches the front of your thighs, helps elongate your quadriceps and increase their flexibility, primes your legs to move into high gear.

QUADRICEPS STRETCH *DO'S* AND *DON'TS*

DON'T sit on your lower legs, leaning back on your hands to stretch your thighs. It places dangerous stress on your knees.

DO stretch from a standing position. Bend one leg straight up behind you, keeping your knees together, grasp the foot with your hand, and pull up gently to give your thigh a good stretch. (You may need to hold on to a wall or chair with your free hand for better balance.)

1-MINUTE LEG SCISSORS

Lie on your back.

Slip your hands under your buttocks to protect your back.

Raise your legs straight up, so that they are perpendicular to the floor.

Open your legs, making as wide a "V" as you can. Keep your legs straight. Bring your legs together, then cross them.

Open, close, and cross for a full minute.

Note: Do not do this exercise if you are prone to lower back pain.

Benefits: Tones your inner and outer thighs, strengthens your lower abdominals.

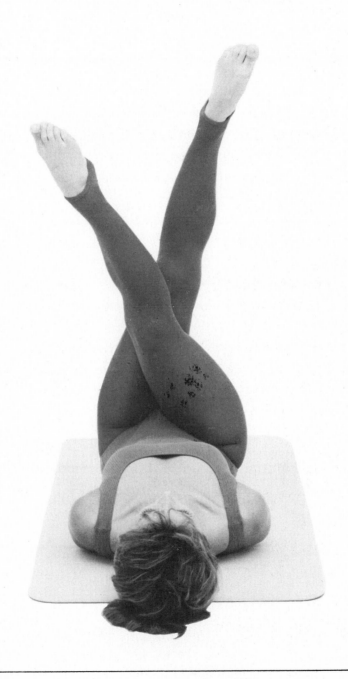

1-MINUTE INNER-THIGH FLAB FIGHTER

Muscles in the inner thighs are often neglected. Even if you jog or run every day, chances are they aren't getting the attention they need—and deserve. I know several people who rarely miss a day of jogging, yet their inner thighs still jiggle and are flabby. If you're one of them, don't despair. Here's an easy way to firm up your inner thighs.

Lie on your back.

Slip your hands under your buttocks, to protect your back.

Raise your legs so that they are perpendicular to the floor.

Bend both knees slightly and place your soles together, turning your knees out so that your legs form a diamond shape.

Take a deep breath, then exhale and slowly pull your feet down and toward your face, pushing your knees further outward.

Inhale, pushing your feet upward again.

Continue moving your feet up and down, pressing the soles together and bending your knees, for a full minute.

Benefits: Strengthens and firms your inner thighs.

1-MINUTE TOWEL STRETCH

After you dry off from a shower, bath, or swim, don't just throw your towel in the laundry hamper or beach bag. Use it to get a good stretch. (I particularly like to do it after I've swum laps for a half hour or so. I sit by the side of the pool and work out the kinks in my legs.)

Sit on the floor or on a mat, with your legs bent.

Loop the towel under the arch of your left foor and grasp both ends.

Straighten your left leg slowly, keeping your back straight and your right foot planted on the floor.

When your leg is fully extended, pull on the ends of the towel. Feel the wonderful stretch in your left calf. (You may feel your arm muscles working, too, as you pull on the ball of your left foot.)

Hold for 20 seconds.

Relax.

Switch legs and repeat.

Variation: Loop the towel under both feet at once and straighten both legs together. Hold and pull for 20 seconds.

Benefits: Stretches your legs, especially your calves; tones your arms.

1-MINUTE STEP/STAIR CALF STRETCH

Eighty percent of American women wear high heels at least twice a week. Even though high heels make your legs look great, they can cause your muscles to tighten from heel to calf and can lead, in turn, to tired, aching legs, ankles, and feet.

I usually wear high heels only for dressy social functions. When my feet begin to hurt, I get relief by slipping away from the crowd and doing this exercise. I don't even have to take off my shoes.

Place the ball of your right foot at the edge of a step.

Press your right heel downward until you feel a stretch in your lower right leg. Hold for 30 seconds.

Release.

Switch legs and repeat.

Benefits: Increases flexibility in your calf muscles and stretches your Achilles tendons.

1-MINUTE CALF AND ACHILLES TENDON STRETCH

This stretch is perfect for shopping and sightseeing expeditions. Instead of walking around with legs that feel heavy and achy, I walk around with legs that are frisky all the time. The next time you're doing a lot of walking around, take 60 seconds now and then to do this stretch because it feels so good.

Stand facing a wall. Place your hands on the wall at shoulder level to support yourself.

Extend your right foot well behind you, bending your left leg. Place both heels flat on the floor.

Lean forward smoothly, pressing your hips toward the wall, until you feel a good stretch in your right calf. Don't bend at the waist. Stretch only as far as you comfortably can; don't bounce.

Hold for 30 seconds.

Release slowly. Stand up straight.

Switch legs. Repeat.

Variation: Try stretching both legs together. Stand a couple of feet away from the wall and place your hands against it for support. Lean forward into the wall until you feel a good stretch. Don't bend at the waist.

Hold for 30 seconds.

Relax. Repeat.

Benefits: Stretches your calves and Achilles tendons, energizes your legs.

1-MINUTE GETTING A LEG UP ON SHIN SPLINTS

When I was competing with the University of Arizona gymnastic team in the late 1970s, I suffered a painful case of shin splints in both legs. Shin splints are a pain in the front or side of the lower leg that occurs when excessive pounding of the legs on hard surfaces—in my case, from tumbling and springboard vaulting—or fallen arches cause muscle to pull away from the shin bone, or when muscles or membranes become inflamed from overuse. Many joggers develop shin splints from jogging on paved roads or concrete or from wearing worn-out shoes that don't adequately absorb shock.

At every university we traveled to that year, I sought advice from the athletic trainer. "Lay off and elevate your feet" was the common exhortation—and "strengthen your arches." I strengthened my arches—with this exercise.

Place a towel flat on the floor in front of a chair. Remove your shoes and socks.

Sit straight in the chair.

Starting at the near edge of the towel, use your toes to roll and gather the towel toward the chair.

Hold the gathered towel for 20 seconds. Release. Repeat twice.

Benefits: Strengthens and builds the arch of your foot, relieves shin splints.

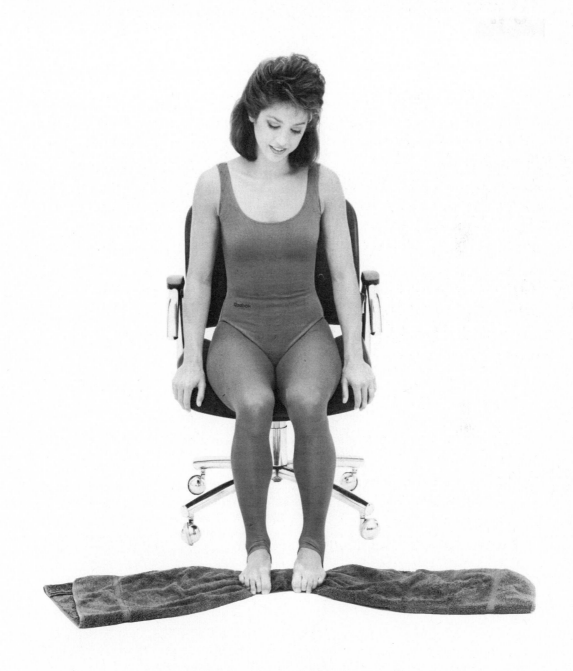

1-MINUTE FOOT MASSAGE

Your poor, aching feet!

Think about them for a while.

You walk on them all the time. You stuff them into shoes that are too tight. You stub them, you get them wet. They get no respect.

When was the last time you soaked them in warm, sudsy water? And sprinkled them with talcum powder? Maybe, just maybe, you rub them at night, but that's not enough. Feet need massaging before they reach the point of exhaustion. All you need is a minute—let's say while you're on hold —and a tennis ball.

Take off your shoes and socks.

Place a tennis ball under one foot.

Roll the ball back and forth under the foot for 30 seconds.

Switch feet and repeat.

Benefits:
Loosens up your feet, and your whole body follows suit.

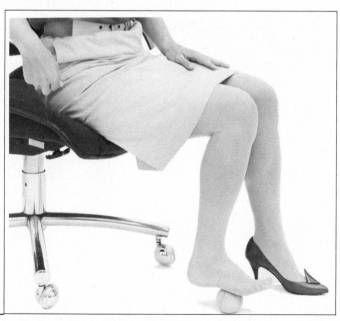

1-MINUTE STANDING-AROUND EXERCISE

If you're on your feet all day, as a salesclerk, say, your feet become far more tired than if you'd been walking all those hours. Standing jams 100 percent of your body weight onto your legs and feet; walking alternates and shifts the load. Standing rigidly and with your knees locked puts extra pressure on your lower back and spine and reduces the flow of blood to your feet. Standing around can also lead to drowsiness, which can make you accident-prone. (One-fourth of all accidents in the industrial workplace are related to fatigue. It's a fact we shouldn't stand for.)

While you're standing on the job, between customers or during a lull—or while you're standing around anywhere—keep your feet in motion.

Roll your insteps in toward each other.
Roll back to a flat stance.
Raise one foot at a time and wiggle your toes.
Stand on your toes as tall as you can.
Settle back onto the soles of your feet.
Repeat for a full minute.

Benefit: Alleviates foot fatigue by stimulating the flow of blood to and in your feet.

WORKOUTS

WHAT IS A WORKOUT?

A workout is 25 percent perspiration and 75 percent determination. Stated another way, it is one part physical exertion and three parts self-discipline. Doing it is easy once you get started.

A workout makes you better today than you were yesterday. It strengthens the body, relaxes the mind, and toughens the spirit. When you work out regularly, your problems diminish and your confidence grows.

A workout is a personal triumph over laziness and procrastination. It is the badge of a winner—the mark of an organized, goal-oriented person who has taken charge of his or her destiny.

A workout is a wise use of time and an investment in excellence. It is a way of preparing for life's challenges and proving to yourself that you have what it takes to do what you need to do.

A workout is a key that helps unlock the door to opportunity and success. Hidden within each of us is an extraordinary force. Physical and mental fitness is the trigger that can release it.

A workout is a form of rebirth. When you finish a good workout, you don't simply feel better, you feel better about yourself.

—George Allen

Exercise isn't an isolated part of your life. How you eat, drink, and rest is essential to your overall health, and in particular to the benefits you derive from working out.

Proper nutrition is essential, particularly if you exercise. Your body needs fuel—the right fuel—to function. (But do wait at least an hour after a full meal before you exercise.) Be sure to drink plenty of water before and after exercise, to prevent dehydration.

Take the time to warm up before you begin to exercise strenuously. Get your blood circulating and give your muscles a thorough stretch. Begin exercising slowly, then work up to a pace your body can handle. Beginners should guard against being over-ambitious; advanced exercisers, against being over-zealous. *Always be true to your body.* Don't try to keep up with friends, classmates, or teachers—their fitness levels and abilities will differ from yours.

Don't exercise outdoors in very cold or very warm weather. In summertime or in hot climates, exercise in the morning or evening, when the temperature is cooler.

Don't skimp on exercise clothing. Wear good-quality shoes that fit well and are designed for the type of exercise you are doing—aerobic, running, and tennis shoes are designed for specific kinds of movement.

If you jog or run, don't use leg weights—they place too much stress on your lower leg and can cause stress-related injuries. Try to avoid running on hard surfaces; if you must run on cement or asphalt, be sure your shoes are in top condition and run slower and take lower steps than usual, to reduce shock. Don't run on paths near congested automobile routes; inhaling exhaust fumes can be as bad for your lungs as cigarette smoking.

Clean your skin before and after you exercise, to help keep your pores unclogged. Dry off with a towel and put on a jacket or sweater before going outdoors in cold weather after exercising.

Take the time to do cool-down exercises after a workout, to help ward off muscle cramps and light-headedness.

WARMING UP TO THE WORKOUT

Muscles, it has been written, are a little like rubber. Stretch a warm rubber band and it gives easily. Stretch a cold rubber band too far and it snaps. So you should warm up even before stretching.

A good warm-up increases the flow of blood and oxygen to your muscles, preparing them gradually for the extra workload to come. Before jumping into a high-intensity workout, you should allot at least 5 to 10 minutes to warming up.

Here are some warm-ups I do before activity.

LOW SKIPS TO INCREASE BLOOD FLOW THROUGH YOUR ENTIRE BODY:

Stand straight.

Lift your right knee high, swinging your left arm forward and your right arm back. Return your foot to the floor.

Lift your left knee, swinging your right arm forward and your left arm back. Return your foot to the floor.

Continue lifting and swinging, alternating legs and arms, 25 times.

LUNGES TO WARM UP YOUR
LEGS AND YOUR UPPER BODY:

Spread your feet wide and lunge to the right, punching the air with your left arm. Be sure that your right knee does not extend beyond your ankle.

Lunge to the left, punching the air with your right arm.

Lunge and punch 30 times, alternating sides.

Be sure you are working your thigh muscles; because they are large, they get more blood pumping and warm you up more quickly. Be careful not to lunge too far, especially if you have knee problems; the knee should not extend past the ankle.

WAIST TWISTS TO INCREASE CIRCULATION THROUGH YOUR TORSO:

Stand with your legs shoulder-width apart, knees slightly bent.

Extend your arms out to the sides and bend your elbows so that your hands point toward the ceiling.

Twist from side to side from the waist, keeping your stomach pulled in, your hips facing forward, your arms at shoulder height.

Do 20 twists.

BACKSTROKES TO INCREASE MOBILITY IN YOUR SHOULDERS AND UPPER BODY:

Stand with your legs shoulder-width apart, your hands at your sides.

Extend your right arm up and back, stretching up on your toes at the farthest point of your reach. Keep your buttocks tight.

Release.

Repeat on the other side.

Continue stretching right and left, up on your toes, 20 times. Pretend you're in the swimming pool, doing the backstroke.

BENT KNEE LIFTS TO
WARM UP YOUR LEGS FULLY:

Stand straight, with your feet slightly apart.

Lift your left knee and try to touch your right elbow to it. Don't lean forward—it's okay if you can't bring your elbow all the way to your knee.

Release.

Lift your right knee and try to touch your left elbow to it.

Release.

Repeat the sequence 20 times, maintaining good posture while in motion.

5-MINUTE WAKE-UP WORKOUT

Good morning, every body.
  Take three good deep breaths.

LET'S WAKE UP YOUR SPINE

Stand with your legs shoulder-width apart, your toes pointing straight ahead.

Stretch your arms overhead and lace your fingers together, palms down. Feel your torso lifting.

Bend your knees slightly.

Bend slowly to the right as far as you comfortably can. Don't bend too far if you have back problems. Keep your hips square and facing forward. Feel the stretch all along your left side. Hold for 10 seconds.

Slowly return to center.

Bend to the left. Hold for 10 seconds.

Return to center.

Repeat the sequence twice.

LET'S WAKE UP YOUR
LEGS, HIPS, AND LOWER BACK

Stand with your feet shoulder-width apart.

Fold your arms directly in front of you.

Bend your knees slightly. Bend forward slowly from the waist, letting your head and folded arms hang loosely.

Hang for 10 seconds, letting gravity loosen your lower back and hamstrings.

Swing your trunk to the right. Hang over your right leg for 10 seconds.

Swing your trunk to the left. Hang over your left leg for 10 seconds. Be sure to keep your knees slightly bent.

Return to center and roll up slowly, one vertebra at a time, keeping your stomach tight.

Note: Skip this one if you have lower back pain.

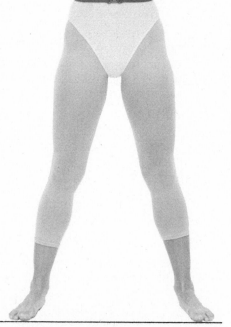

LET'S WAKE UP
YOUR HEART AND LUNGS

Stand with your feet shoulder-width apart.

Link your fingers behind your head.

Lift your left knee and touch your right elbow to it. Return your left foot to the floor.

Lift your right knee and touch your left elbow to it.

Continue, alternating knees and elbows, as often as you can for 30 seconds. Increase oxygen delivery to your muscles and snap yourself awake by exhaling through your mouth quickly and forcefully as you move.

LET'S WAKE UP YOUR
ARMS, CHEST, AND SHOULDERS

Do two kinds of push-ups—with your fingers pointed forward for 30 seconds, then for 30 seconds more with your fingers pointed inward toward each other. (See 1-Minute Beautiful Biceps, p. 62.)

LET'S WAKE UP YOUR BELLY

Lie on your back, with your knees bent.

Rest your right foot on your left knee and extend your right knee out to the side.

Place your fingertips behind your ears and push your elbows back.

Lift your shoulders slowly off the mat, as high as you can. Look straight up at the ceiling.

Hold for 10 seconds.

Release.

Switch legs and repeat.

Repeat twice more, alternating legs.

Jump up! You're awake!

5- AND 10-MINUTE HEALTHY BACK PROGRAMS

To have a healthy back, you must have healthy back and abdominal muscles. And you must also maintain adequate strength and flexibility in the muscles and joints of the hips—in the hip flexors and extensors in particular. Your hip flexors allow you to raise your knees and sit; the extensors let you straighten your hips and legs. Both come into play when, for example, you kick a football.

If you want to ward off a bad back, you may want to do this program every day. If you have a bad back, consult your physician first. (If you have problems with your back, you should seek medical attention in any case.)

ELIMINATING BACKACHE

Experts estimate that up to one-third of lower back injuries for which worker's compensation is paid could be eliminated by improving chair designs and by teaching employees "back-saving" ways of doing their jobs. Backaches, in fact, are second only to head colds as the leading cause of time lost from work. Back pain can make even an easy task like tying your shoelaces a "backbreaking" task.

Having a healthy, strong, pain-free back is important to overall good health. But don't get your back up waiting for the boss to go out to buy you a new chair. Learn to compensate for a less-than-perfect chair.

continued

continued

> **Put a firm pillow against the back of your chair to support your lower back.**
>
> **Prop up one foot—on a stool or an ottoman or a pile of books. (When one knee is higher than your hips, the pressure on your spine is greatly reduced.)**
>
> **Sit up straight. Don't slump!**
>
> **Distribute your weight evenly on both buttocks.**
>
> **Avoid crossing your legs.**
>
> **Try to lean forward from your hips when you work, instead of rounding your back and shoulders.**
>
> **Stand for a couple of minutes at least once every hour. Take time to do some 1-minute stretches.**

5-MINUTE PROGRAM

SIDE SLIDES

Stand with your feet shoulder-width apart, knees slightly bent and hands at your sides.

Bend to the right from the waist, sliding your right hand slowly down the outside of your right thigh until you reach a point of tension. Slide your hand as close to your right knee as you can without straining. Feel the stretch along your left side. Hold for 15 seconds.

Slowly return to the starting position, sliding your hand back up your thigh.

Repeat on the left side.

Note: If one side feels less flexible than the other, concentrate on that side and hold the stretch a few seconds longer. Tightness on one side can strain the spine and can lead to pinched nerves.

Benefits: Warms up your back, waist, and hips, increases overall flexibility.

POSTURE STRETCH

Stand with your feet shoulder-width apart.

Lace your fingers in front of you, arms straight, palms in, and raise your arms straight up over your head. Extend your body fully until you feel a good stretch (but no strain). Lift your torso and rib cage. Do not bend at the waist or arch your back; let your upper body do the work.

Hold for 10 seconds. Release. Repeat 2 times.

Benefits: Increases flexibility in your arms, chest, and shoulders; improves posture, crucial for a healthy back.

GRAVITY HANG

Stand with your feet shoulder-width apart, knees slightly bent.

Bend forward slowly, rounding your back one vertebra at a time. Let your head and arms hang loose, like a rag doll's. Hang for 30 seconds, letting gravity stretch the muscles of your lower back and your hamstrings; don't bounce. Breathe naturally.

Roll up slowly, one vertebra at a time, keeping your stomach tight and your chin tucked in to your chest. Stand tall.

Benefits: Stretches your lower back and hamstrings, relieves pressure on and tension in your lower back.

BACK PRESS

Lie on your back on a carpet or mat, with your knees bent and your feet planted on the floor. Hold your arms at your sides, palms down.

Tighten your abdominal muscles, squeeze your buttocks together, and slowly press the small of your back into the floor.

Hold for 15 seconds.

Relax.

Repeat 3 times.

Benefits: Stretches your back and strengthens your abdominal muscles, relieves pressure on your lower back and thus helps prevent sway-back.

BUTTOCK STRETCH

Lie on your back on a carpet or mat, knees bent, feet planted on the floor.

Raise your right foot and plant it on your left knee. Extend your right knee out to the side.

Holding this position, grasp your knees with your hands and bring them slowly to your chest. Feel the stretch in your right buttock.

Hold for 15 seconds. Release.

Switch legs and repeat.

Repeat the sequence on each side.

Benefits: Stretches your buttocks, alleviates strain on your pelvis and lower back.

10-MINUTE PROGRAM

Do the 5-minute program above first, then continue with the following:

LOWER BACK STRETCH

Lie flat on your back on a carpet or mat, knees bent, feet flat on the floor.

Tighten your tummy muscles and bring your right knee in to your chest, grasping the back of your thigh with both hands just above the knee. Press the small of your back to the floor. Breathe normally. Feel the stretch in your lower back. Hold for 15 seconds.

Switch legs and repeat.

Release.

Bring both knees in to your chest. Raise your head. Press the small of your back against the floor. Hold for 15 seconds. Release.

Relax.

Benefits: Stretches and relaxes your lower back, increases flexibility.

TUMMY TIGHTENER

Lie on your back on a carpet or mat with both knees bent, feet flat on the floor.

Raise your left foot and place it on your right knee. Relax your left knee out to the side.

Place your fingertips behind your ears and press your elbows back. Flatten the small of your back against the floor, tilting your pelvis.

Using your abdominal muscles, lift your head and shoulders off the floor. Keep your chin up and your eyes on the ceiling. Exhale through your mouth. (Don't hold your breath.)

Hold this position for 15 seconds. (If you are a beginner, it may take you a while to work up to a 15-second hold; try starting with three 5-second holds.)

Relax.

Repeat.

Switch legs and repeat the sequence.

Benefits: Works your abdominal muscles, builds a strong base of support for your back, helps to prevent back pain and injury.

TORSO TONER

Lie on your back on a carpet or mat.

Bend your knees and keep them together. Extend your arms straight out to the side. (If your back needs extra support, tuck your hands under your buttocks.)

Pull your knees in to your chest and roll them together to the floor on your right. Hold for 10 seconds.

Roll your knees back across your body to the floor on your left. Be sure that your shoulders stay flat and your stomach stays tucked. Hold for 10 seconds.

Repeat 2 times.

Benefits:
Strengthens the sides of your torso (the internal and external oblique muscles), relaxes your lower back.

TRUNK EXTENSION

Lie on your stomach on a carpet or mat, with your feet about 6 inches apart.

Clasp your hands behind your head and press your elbows back.

Exhale and raise your head and upper chest slowly off the floor. Keep your hips, legs, and feet on the floor. Squeeze your buttock muscles.

Hold for 10 seconds.

Relax for 10 seconds.

Hold. Relax. Hold. Relax.

Release.

Benefits: Strengthens your back extensors, the muscles that support your back and keep your spinal column in alignment; firms your buttocks and thighs.

BACK RELAXER AND COOL-DOWN

Kneel on the floor, with your buttocks resting on your heels.

Place your hands on the floor in front of your knees.

Slide your hands forward slowly, lowering your head between your arms and relaxing your neck. Stretch your arms as far out as possible along the floor.

Hold for a full minute, breathing deeply.

Benefits: Increases back and hip flexibility, reduces pressure on your back (especially from fatigue and emotional tension), cools you down.

10-MINUTE TONE-UP WALK

"Walking has the best value of gymnastics of the mind."
—*Ralph Waldo Emerson*

Walking tones your muscles and strengthens your heart. Even a stroll burns calories. Power walkers really burn off the fat as they roar along at top speed—120 steps per minute. If you take 50 steps every walking minute, you're in good walking shape. But don't overdo it; if you can't talk normally while you're walking (or running, for that matter), you're pushing yourself too hard. Slow down. (Talking with a friend helps keep you in a healthy stride.)

Let's stride into shape. Put your best foot forward, and keep your head up, your chest high. Try these variations as you walk—a full minute each— and breathe rhythmically, exhaling forcefully.

WARM-UP WALK

Walk normally, to warm up your body and loosen your joints.

STRIDE STRETCH

Take long strides, stretching your thighs and calves. Swing your arms to get your heart pumping and to increase circulation.

ARMS UP ALTERNATELY

Walk at a brisk pace.

Punch the air overhead, first with your right arm, then with your left. Punch with your right as you step with your left leg, punch with your left as you step with your right. Feel your rib cage lifting. Exhale with each punch.

ARMS PUNCH FRONT ALTERNATELY

Keep up a brisk walking pace.

Punch straight ahead with your fists. Shadowbox. When you step forward with your right foot, punch with your left fist and draw your right arm back; when you step with your left foot, punch with your right fist and draw your left arm back. Keep your arms parallel to the ground. Feel the stretch in your upper back. Keep your abdominals tight.

TRICEPS TONER

Continue walking briskly.

Place both arms behind your back, keeping them straight, palms turned back.

Scissor your arms behind your back as you walk.

ARM CURLS

Keep walking at a brisk pace.

Hold your arms close to your body. Bend your elbows and extend your forearms straight in front of you, palms up, as if you were carrying a tray with both hands. Make fists with both hands.

Bring your fists in to your chest as you walk, working your biceps. Lower your fists to the extended position. Continue raising and lowering your arms, up, down, up, down, maintaining resistance in both directions as you walk.

ARM FLAPS

Keep up your pace. Extend your arms out to the sides.
Maintaining resistance, bring your arms together straight overhead.

Lower your arms to your sides, then raise them overhead. Raise, lower, in rhythm with your stride. Keep your arms straight and the muscles tight. Turn your palms up as you raise your arms, down as you lower your arms, to take advantage of air resistance.

CHEST FIRMER

"We must, we must, we *must* expand our bust." I remember hearing that exhortation repeatedly from my high school phys ed teacher.

You're still walking briskly, right? And exhaling forcefully?

Extend your arms to the side; elbows bent so that your fingers point toward the sky.

Bring your forearms together in front of your chest, maintaining resistance.

Press your arms back out again, keeping the muscles tight.

Press together, apart, together, apart as you walk.

ARM SCISSORS

Continue to walk briskly, taking long strides.

Extend your arms straight out to the sides.

Crisscross your arms in front of your chest, keeping them straight, maintaining resistance.

Press your arms to the sides again, as wide as you can.

Continue to cross and open, cross and open, as you walk. Cross with first your right arm, then your left, on top, maintaining resistance in both directions.

STRIDE IT OUT

Take long strides with long arm swings—move naturally.

Start slowing down, taking it easy.

Stop moving and relax.

Don't you feel super?

Benefits: Conditions your cardiovascular system; tones your upper body, stomach, buttocks, and legs; brings a smile to your face.

5-MINUTE ABOVE-THE-BELT WORKOUT

Let's firm up the upper body, working over your upper arms, upper back, chest, shoulders—the whole upper torso. Turn flab to firm—no more saggy, dingle-dangle arms or slouching shoulders—by doing this program every day.

SHOULDER/POSTURE STRETCH

Stand comfortably, with your feet shoulder-width apart.

Raise your arms up and back in full circles. Rotate them slowly but continuously for 30 seconds. Keep your arms taut, your tummy tight, and your back straight—don't arch.

Release.

Rotate your arms in the other direction, again making exaggerated circles, for 30 seconds.

Relax.

Benefits: Increases flexibility in your shoulders, improves overall posture, circulation, flexibility.

UPPER ARM TONER

Stand straight with your feet slightly apart.

Extend your arms overhead, palms touching, then bend them back at a 90-degree angle so that your fingers point straight back behind your head. Your elbows should be close to your head, and the heels of your hands should be directly in line with your spine.

Keeping your hands pressed together and your arm muscles tight, lower your hands about 3 inches, maintaining resistance.

Press your arms back up.

Continue to press down and up, down and up for 30 seconds, keeping your back straight and your arms close to your head.

Relax.

Benefit: Works your pectorals and triceps.

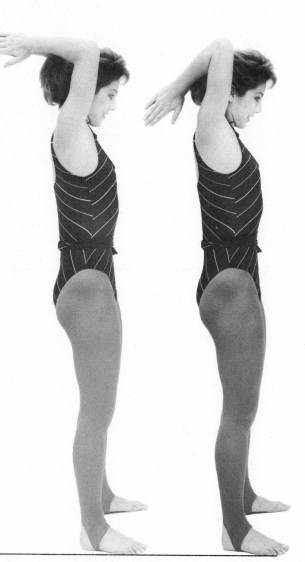

CHEST LIFTS

The muscles of your chest—the pectorals—work in harmony with the muscles of your arms, shoulders, and back to help keep your chest lifted. Exercise will not actually enlarge a woman's breasts, but it can help to support her bosom, which will make her chest seem larger.

Stand comfortably, with your feet shoulder-width apart.

Bring your palms and forearms together in front of your chest, with your arms at right angles and your upper arms parallel to the floor—in an exaggerated attitude of prayer.

Hold for 30 seconds, pressing your forearms and hands together. Be sure you continue to inhale and exhale at a normal rate. Feel the muscles of your arms and chest working.

Benefits: Develops, conditions, and strengthens your chest muscles.

UPPER BACK FIRMER

Stand comfortably, with your feet shoulder-width apart.

Extend your arms straight out to the sides. Bend your elbows at right angles, so that your fingers point toward the ceiling and your palms face forward.

Bring your forearms and hands together in front of your chest, working against resistance.

Press your arms back out to the sides again, as far as you comfortably can.

Press together, apart, together, apart continuously for 60 seconds, maintaining resistance in both directions.

Benefits: Conditions and strengthens the muscles of your chest and upper back.

UPPER TORSO CONDITIONER

Assume a push-up starting position (*men* on their hands and the balls of the feet, body aligned from head to toe; *women* on their hands and knees, body aligned from head to knee). Place your hands directly beneath your shoulders, fingers pointing forward.

Lift your right leg off the floor and bend it up behind you in a right angle.

Bend your arms, lowering your body almost to the floor, keeping your body aligned.

Slowly straighten your arms and return to the starting position. Be sure your body stays straight!

Do as many of these push-ups as you can in 30 seconds.

Relax.

Switch legs and repeat.

Benefits: Conditions and strengthens your upper torso—arms, chest, and shoulders.

5-MINUTE ROCK-HARD TUMMY

Go from fat to flat with this stomach-slimming, waistline-trimming workout. I do it every day!

TORSO TRIMMER

Stand with your feet a little more than shoulder-width apart, toes turned out as in a *plié* position.

Bend your knees to a 45-degree angle, keeping your derriere tucked under. (Your feet should be far enough apart that your knees do not extend past your ankles.)

Lace your fingers behind your head and extend your elbows out to the sides.

Exhale and bend sideways to the right from the waist. Try to touch your right elbow to your right knee. (Don't bend too far if it bothers your back.)

Return to center and inhale.

Bend to the left. Try to touch your left elbow to your left knee.

Return to center.

Continue bending from side to side for 60 seconds. Remember to breathe and to keep your derriere tucked under. Bend straight to the side; don't hunch.

B e n e f i t s : Trims and tones the sides of your waist, helps get rid of any love handles at the back of your waist.

FRONT TUMMY TIGHTENER

Lie on your back on a carpet or mat, with both knees bent and feet flat on the floor.

Raise your left foot and place it on your right knee. Relax your left knee out to the side.

Place your fingertips behind your ears and press your elbows back. Press the small of your back against the floor.

Lift your head and shoulders slowly off the floor—no more than 4 inches or so—using your abdominal muscles. Keep your chin up and your eyes fixed on the ceiling. Exhale through your mouth as you lift—don't hold your breath.

Hold for 15 seconds.

Lower yourself to the floor, one vertebra at a time.

Relax.

Switch legs and repeat.

Repeat on both sides.

Benefit: Works your entire abdominal region, including the rectus abdominis, the long muscle running vertically along the abdominal wall from your chest bone to your pubic bone.

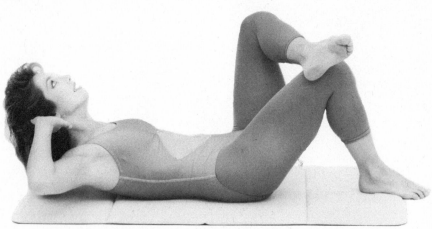

SIDE TUMMY TRIMMER

Lie on your back on a carpet or mat, knees bent and feet flat on the floor.
Lace your fingers behind your head and press your elbows back.
Raise your right foot and place it on your left knee.
Slowly raise your head and shoulders from the floor. Exhale and twist to
the right from your waist. Try to touch your left elbow to your right knee.
Keep your right elbow on the floor. (Don't fret if you can't touch your knee;
reaching toward it works your tummy muscles plenty.)
Slowly lower your head and shoulders to the floor.
Continue lifting, twisting, and lowering for 30 seconds.
Release.
Switch sides and repeat, twisting your right elbow to your left knee.

Benefits: Tones and strengthens your internal and external obliques,
the muscles along the sides and front of your abdomen; trims your
waistline.

REVERSE SIT-UPS

Lie on your back on a carpet or mat, knees bent.

Place your arms at your sides, palms down. (If your back needs support, tuck your hands under your buttocks.)

Bring your knees up and in toward your chin, using your abdominal muscles. Your buttocks will come off the floor as your pelvis tucks up.

Lower your buttocks to the floor but keep your legs up and your knees bent.

Continue to raise and lower your buttocks as often as you can for a full minute, pulling your knees as close in to your chin as possible. Use your abdominals; don't rely on momentum.

Benefits: Strengthens your lower abdominals, helps diminish a protruding tummy.

TOTAL TUMMY SLIMMER

Lie on your back on a carpet or mat, knees bent.

Press the small of your back to the floor.

Bring your right knee in to your chest and grasp the knee with both hands; keep your elbows out to the sides. (If you have knee problems, grasp behind your thigh.) Extend your left leg straight out, a couple of inches off the floor. Don't arch your spine.

Lift your head and shoulders off the floor, contracting your abdominal muscles.

Switch legs—bend your left, extend your right.

Continue to alternate legs for a full minute, keeping your head and shoulders and your heels off the floor the entire time, pressing the small of your back to the floor.

Relax.

N o t e : Be careful with this one if you have neck or shoulder problems.

B e n e f i t s : Tones your abdominal muscles, fights teddy-bear tummy.

LEG RAISES *DO'S*
AND *DON'TS*

DON'T let your lower back come off the floor. It places a terrible strain on your lower back.

DO raise your head and shoulders slightly off the ground and keep your spine pressed to the floor. Place your hands under your buttocks for added support. Raise and lower one leg at a time, bending your opposite knee in toward your chest.

5-MINUTE HOT LEGS WORKOUT

Everyone would like to love his or her own legs, and to have them the cynosure of all eyes. Here's how you can develop strength and tone in your legs that can maximize their attractiveness and athletic capabilities.

TONER

Stand with your feet far apart—wider than shoulder-width, knees and toes turned out as in a *plié* position.

Place your hands on your hips and bend your knees slowly. Try to bend your legs to a 90-degree angle. Be sure that your pelvis stays tucked under —don't arch—and that your knees do not extend past your ankles. Tighten your abdominal muscles.

Hold this position for 30 seconds.

Pulse up and down very slightly—only about 3 inches—for an additional 30 seconds, keeping your knees bent.

Note: Skip this exercise if you have had knee problems.

Benefits: Tones your thighs, especially the quadriceps; warms up your legs and your body overall for a good workout.

HEEL LIFTS

Stand with your feet a little more than shoulder-width apart.

Bend forward from the waist and place your palms on the floor. "Walk" your hands out to at least 12 inches in front of your feet. Keep your stomach muscles tight and relax your head and neck.

Slowly lift your heels off the floor so that you're on the balls of your feet. Exhale as you push up, contracting your abdominal muscles even further.

Slowly lower your heels to the floor.

Continue to lift and lower your heels—slowly, keeping your legs slightly straight—for 30 seconds. Feel the stretch along the backs of your lower legs —in the calf muscles and Achilles tendons.

Variation: Assume the starting position described above, but point your toes in toward each other. Keep your heels flat and hold for 30 seconds. Feel a great stretch along the outside of your lower legs.

Note: If you have trouble bending over, stand facing a wall, about 12 inches away. Lean your body against the wall, supporting yourself with your palms. Perform heel lifts as above.

Benefits: Stretches and strengthens your calf muscles; helps avoid injuries to your lower leg.

SADDLEBAG TRIMMER

Lie on your right side on a carpet or mat, with your torso raised and your weight resting on your right forearm. Keep your legs straight and your body aligned.

Flex your feet and raise your left leg.

Lower the leg smoothly, keeping the muscles taut.

Lift and lower for 30 seconds. Use your abdominal muscles to help maintain proper form.

Switch sides and repeat, raising and lowering your right leg.

Benefits: Tones the outsides of your thighs, firms up saddlebags.

INNER THIGH LIFT

Lie on your right side on a carpet or mat, with your torso raised and supported on your right forearm. Keep your legs straight and your body aligned.

Lift your left leg straight up and grasp the calf with your left hand.

Try to bring your right leg up to meet the left. Use your abdominals to keep your body aligned, so that your right inner thigh faces the ceiling and gets a good workout as you raise your leg.

Lower your right leg to the floor, keeping your left leg raised.

Lift and lower your right leg for 30 seconds.

Switch sides and repeat, bringing your left leg up to meet your raised right leg.

Note: If you find this exercise too difficult, try bending your left leg and placing the heel flat on the floor in front of your right knee. Lift and lower your right leg as above. Switch sides and repeat.

Benefits: Tones and trims your inner thighs, gets rid of the "jiggles."

REAR THIGH TRIMMER

Get down on your knees and forearms on a carpet or mat.

Extend your left leg straight out behind you and point your toes.

Lift your left leg as high as you can, keeping it straight. Work the muscles of your left thigh and derriere. Concentrate on good form—don't arch your back or swing or jerk your leg up.

Lower your leg smoothly.

Lift and lower for 30 seconds, keeping your movements controlled. Think good form.

Release.

Switch legs and repeat.

Note: Be careful with this one if you have lower back pain.

Benefits: Tones and trims the back of your thighs, firms your buttocks.

Stand up. Pat yourself on the back. Good going!

REAR THIGH LIFT *DO'S* AND *DON'TS*

DON'T extend your leg toward the ceiling, arching your spine and locking your elbows.

DO place your forearms on the floor and extend one leg straight back. Relax your neck and keep your head and back straight. Lift your leg straight up, without bending it.

5- AND 10-MINUTE REV-IT-UPS

Have you ever arrived home from work dead tired and had to change your clothes in a hurry and rush out to a dinner or a cocktail party—but were so bushed that you really just wanted to hit the sack? Who hasn't! These exercises will give you such a boost that you'll want to dance all night. Do them in sequence, each one for a full minute. Get going!

5-MINUTE PROGRAM

BODY PUMP

Stand with your legs shoulder-width apart, your knees slightly bent.

Extend your arms out to the sides, and bend your elbows so that your hands point toward the ceiling. Make fists.

Straighten your legs and extend your left arm straight overhead. Reach as high as you can, using your leg muscles.

Lower your arm and bend your knees.

Extend your right arm overhead, straightening and pushing from your legs.

Bend, extend, bend, extend, pumping away as you alternate arms.

Benefits: Gets your blood and oxygen pumping, gives you a good overall stretch.

TWIST AND PUMP

Stand with your legs shoulder-width apart, your knees slightly bent.

Assume a fighting stance: Cock your fists at your shoulders and extend your elbows out to the sides.

Twist to the left and punch in that direction with your right fist, extending your arm as far as you can. Lift your right heel to allow you to extend your right leg fully. Use your leg muscles!

Twist and punch to the right, extending your left arm and lifting your left heel.

Continue twisting left and right, punching right and left, for a full minute.

Benefits: Warms up your whole body, trims your midriff, gives a good stretch along your waistline to eliminate love handles.

LEG PUMPS

Sit on a carpet or mat with your legs extended straight in front of you.
Lean back and rest on your elbows.
Raise your legs slightly off the floor.
"Bicycle" your legs in the air for a full minute, alternately pulling your knees in to your chest. Keep your abdominal muscles firm—it'll make it easier to support your legs. Be sure that the small of your back stays pressed against the floor. (If this exercise causes too much strain on your lower back, lie back and place your hands under your buttocks for support as you bicycle.)

Benefits: Tones and strengthens your legs and tummy muscles, helps eliminate belly bulge.

LEG SCISSORS

Lie on your back on a carpet or mat.

Place your palms flat on the floor under your buttocks for support.

Raise your legs straight overhead, perpendicular to the floor. Point your toes.

Keeping your legs straight and taut, open them as wide as you can. Feel a wonderful stretch in your inner thighs.

Bring your legs together and cross them.

Continue crisscrossing your legs for a full minute. Pull in and contract your abdominal muscles to keep your movements precise and controlled.

Benefits: Increases flexibility in your thighs, tones and trims them—especially the inner-thigh "trouble spots"—into bathing-suit shape.

THE PERFECT PUSH-UP

Do 30 seconds of push-ups with your fingers pointing forward—men from the balls of their feet, women from their knees. Then turn your fingers inward and do push-ups for 30 seconds more. (For instructions and pictures, see Beautiful Biceps, p. 62.)

10-MINUTE PROGRAM

Do the 5-minute program above first, then continue with the following:

LOWER TUMMY TIGHTENER

This one is a little advanced, so be patient as you do it.

Sit on a carpet or mat.

Place your palms on the floor, just behind your buttocks, with the fingers pointing forward. Lean back slightly, bending your elbows.

Bend your knees and bring them in to your chest, raising your feet off the ground.

Extend your legs straight out in front of you, using your abdominals to keep them off the floor and to control the movement.

Pull your legs back in to your chest, then extend them again. Pull in, extend, pull in, extend. Try to do 30 repetitions in a minute. Be sure to use your arms to take stress off your lower back. And don't let your feet touch the floor!

B e n e f i t s : Flattens your abdomen, particularly the lower abdomen; strengthens your quadriceps.

PELVIC TILTS

Lie on your back on a carpet or mat, with your knees bent and your feet flat on the floor, about hip-width apart. Place your hands at your sides, palms down.

Concentrate on relaxing and elongating your neck muscles.

Squeeze your buttocks and your abdominal muscles, then tuck your pelvis up, until your buttocks are slightly off the floor. Keep your head, shoulders, torso, and feet pressed against the floor.

Hold the pelvic tilt for 10 seconds.

Roll back down to the floor slowly, vertebra by vertebra.

Relax.

Repeat 5 times.

Benefit: Firms your fanny and lower abdomen.

HIP SLIMMER

Lie on your right side on a carpet or mat.

Raise your torso and support yourself on your right forearm.

Bend your right leg back along the floor behind your body.

Extend your left leg straight out to the front and flex the foot.

Raise your left foot several inches off the floor and circle it forward 10 times.

Circle your foot backward 10 times. Don't let it touch the floor!

Switch sides and repeat, circling your right foot.

Benefit: Slims your hips and outer thighs.

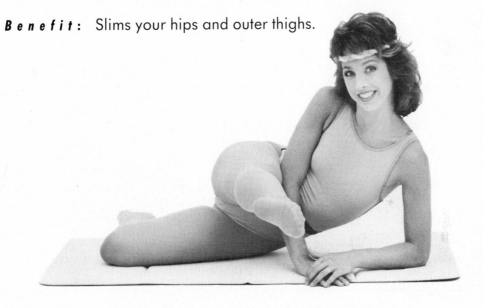

INNER THIGH LIFT

Follow the instructions in the 5-Minute Hot Legs Workout, page 184.

THIGH STRETCH

Lie flat on your tummy on a carpet or mat.

Extend your arms straight out in front of you along the floor.

Bend your right leg up behind you, keeping the thigh flat on the floor. Reach back with your right hand and grasp your right ankle. Pull your foot gently toward your buttocks, keeping your knee in line with your body (don't let it jut out to the side). Feel a good stretch in the front of your thigh.

Hold for 30 seconds. Release.

Repeat the stretch on your left side.

B e n e f i t : Stretches your quadriceps.

The biggest benefit of all: You're pumped up for a night on the town!

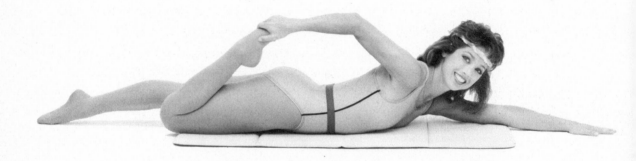

10-MINUTE PARTNER WORKOUT

Working out need not be an individual pursuit. Shaping up with another person introduces added pleasure, and it's a great way to share a health-improving activity with your spouse, child, or best friend.

As a teenager, I was fortunate to warm up with the Japanese men's and women's Olympic gymnastic teams when they visited Los Angeles for exhibitions with American teams. Many of the stretching exercises I learned from the Japanese are performed with a partner. Even if the two of you differ in size, weight, age, or gender, both of you will benefit.

Your partner can help you reach your maximum stretch without bouncing or jerking. Like a weight machine, your partner can provide you with resistance—and he or she gets a workout at the same time! My 10-Minute Partner Workout is a combination of stretching for flexibility and conditioning for strength and tone. You don't have to limit yourselves to 10 minutes—or to my routine, for that matter. Experiment, find new ways to exercise together. Grab your partner and let's go.

PARTNER SQUAT

Stand facing each other at about arm's length, knees slightly bent. Clasp hands.

Lean back just enough to support each other's weight.

Bend your knees, lowering yourselves to a sitting position. Be careful not to bend your knees past a 90-degree angle. Keep your back straight.

Hold for 1 minute. Don't let go!

Note : Skip this exercise if you have knee problems.

Benefits : Strengthens and tones thigh muscles, provides a fine warm-up.

UPPER-BODY TOWEL TONER

Hold a bath towel at one end with both hands.

Stand with your back straight and your feet comfortably apart.

Gripping the towel, raise your arms overhead. Bend your forearms back at right angles, so that the towel hangs down behind you.

Have your partner grasp the towel behind your neck and gently pull down on it as you pull up.

Tug against your partner's resistance for 30 seconds. Don't forget to breathe normally!

Switch roles and repeat.

Benefits: Tones your arms and shoulders, especially the triceps; helps eliminate underarm flab.

PARTNER SIT-UPS

Lie on your back on a carpet or mat, knees bent, feet flat on the floor.
Have your partner sit at your feet and grasp your calves or ankles.

Cross your arms over your chest and raise your torso off the ground,
coming halfway to a sitting position, as your partner restrains your feet.
Don't let your partner do the work, though!

Do as many sit-ups as you can in 30 seconds.

Switch roles and repeat.

Benefits: Strengthens the abdominal muscles, flattens the stomach.

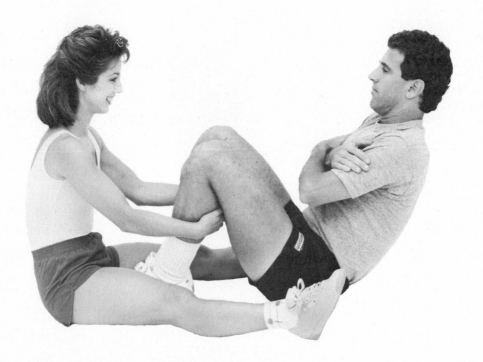

PARTNER SHOULDER STRETCH

Sit on the floor, legs folded in front of you, with your partner standing behind you.

Extend your arms behind you, keeping your back straight.

Have your partner grasp your wrists and pull them gently upward, only as far as is comfortable, and hold them there for 10 seconds.

Have your partner bring your hands together behind you and crisscross them alternately, lowering them very slowly. (This should take at least 20 seconds.) Be careful not to lean too far forward.

Switch roles and repeat.

Benefits: Increases flexibility and releases tension in your arms, chest, and shoulders.

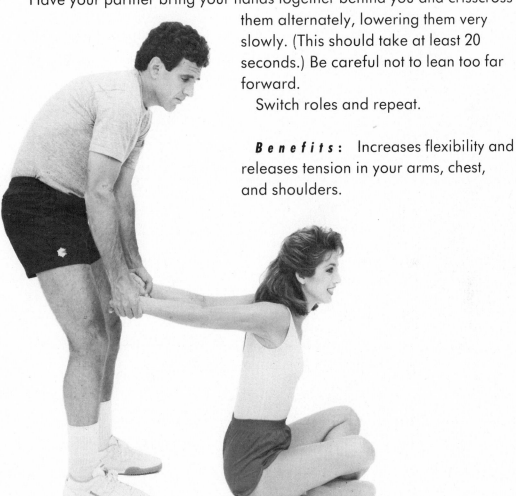

OLYMPIC POSTURE/STRETCH MINIMASSAGE

Sit on the floor, legs extended comfortably in front of you, back straight.

Lace your fingers behind your neck and extend your elbows out to the sides.

Have your partner stand behind you and press your elbows back gently with his or her palms, as far as is comfortable for you.

Hold for 20 seconds. (I like my partner to place a knee in the center of my back, between my shoulder blades, for extra support and stability.)

Have your partner release you slowly.

Here's the fun part: Have your partner give you a mini–shoulder massage for 10 seconds.

Switch roles and repeat.

Benefits: Stretches your pectoral muscles, improves posture, revitalizes you.

PARTNER LEG STRETCHES

Sit on the floor, back straight, your legs straddled in front of you as far as is comfortable. Turn your toes toward the ceiling.

Have your partner kneel behind you.

Lean forward, extending your arms straight in front of you along the floor.

Have your partner push gently on your lower back until you reach a comfortable point of tension.

Hold for 30 seconds. Take deep, slow breaths and relax.

Switch roles and repeat.

B e n e f i t : Increases flexibility in the inner thigh, groin, and lower back.

PARTNER LEG PRESSES

Sit on the floor—both of you—and face each other.

Place your hands on the floor behind you and lean back, with your elbows slightly bent.

Bend your knees and raise your legs. Place the soles of your feet against your partner's soles. Press hard against each other.

Hold for 20 seconds, maintaining resistance.

Relax.

Repeat twice.

Benefits: Strengthens legs and abdominal muscles, especially the quadriceps.

INNER/OUTER THIGH TONER

Sit on the floor facing each other.

Place your hands on the floor and lean back, bending your elbows.

Raise your legs to at least a 45-degree angle, keeping them straight. Place your ankles inside your partner's ankles. Flex your feet (all four of them).

Press out while your partner presses in, resisting each other, for 30 seconds.

Relax.

Switch positions—place your ankles outside your partner's. Press again for 30 seconds.

Be careful that neither of you presses the other beyond a comfortable point.

Benefits: Firms and strengthens your inner and outer thighs and your buttocks.

PARTNER LEG CURLS

Lie on your stomach, preferably on a carpet or mat, your chin resting on your arms, with a folded towel under your knees.

Have your partner kneel beside you and grasp your ankles.

Bend your legs slowly, bringing your heels toward your buttocks, feet flexed, legs 6 to 8 inches apart, as your partner provides resistance.

Lower your legs slowly while your partner continues to maintain resistance. Continue for 30 seconds, being careful not to let your partner exert more pressure than is comfortable for you. Keep your hips flat on the floor and your spine straight—don't arch.

Switch roles and repeat.

Benefits: Firms and strengthens hamstrings and quadriceps.

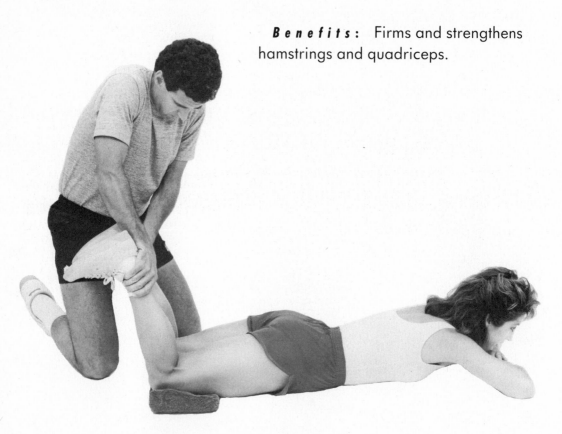

DOUBLE COOL-DOWN

Stand side by side, about 2 feet apart.

Raise your arms over your heads.

Bend sideways toward each other and join hands, inner hands clasping at hip level, outer hands clasping overhead. Lean out at the hips. Feel the stretch in your arms and shoulders and in the sides of your waist.

Hold for 30 seconds.

Hands still clasped, turn in toward each other and then out again, facing the opposite direction. Lean out and stretch the other side. Hold for 30 seconds.

Benefits: Provides a good overall stretch, especially at the sides of the waist and hips and through the arms, shoulders, and back.

You did it!
Give your partner a big hug.

5-MINUTE GOOD NIGHT, SLEEP TIGHT ROUTINE

Bathe. Brush your teeth. Comb your hair. Ready?

SPINAL ROLL

Sit on the edge of your bed, spine straight. Plant your feet on the floor, shoulder-width apart.

Drop your chin to your chest (don't force it!). Feel the stretch in your neck. Hold for 10 seconds.

Bend forward slowly from the waist, curving your spine and letting your head and arms hang loosely, until your chest touches your thighs.

Relax like a rag doll for 10 seconds.

Tighten your abdominal muscles and roll up slowly, one vertebra at a time. Feel your spine elongate.

Repeat the sequence.

B e n e f i t s : Helps maintain spinal flexibility, relieves spinal pressure and compression.

LEG STRETCH

Lie flat on your back on your bed, with your head on your pillow. Relax.

Pull your right knee in to your chest and grasp it with both hands. (If you have knee problems, grasp your thigh behind the knee instead.) Keep your left leg extended straight on the bed and your back flat.

Hold for 15 seconds.

Extend your right leg straight up, grasp it behind the knee, and pull it toward you as far as you comfortably can without bending it. Feel the stretch in the back of your leg.

Hold for 15 seconds.

Release. Relax.

Repeat the stretch with the left leg.

Benefits: Stretches your hamstrings, eases lower back tension.

LEG STRETCH *DO'S*
AND *DON'TS*

DON'T raise or turn your hip in order to bring your leg closer in to your chest. Not only does this nullify any benefits of the exercise, but it also places undue stress on your lower back.

DO keep your hips flat on the floor and grasp your leg with both hands. Straighten your leg and pull it toward your chest until you feel a good stretch in the back of the thigh.
It is not important that you bring
your leg all the way in to your chest
or that you grasp it down at the calf.
It is important to keep your hips
flat on the floor.

LEGS UP

Lie flat on your back on a firm mattress with your head on a pillow, knees bent.

Raise your feet off the mattress and bring both knees in to your chest, hugging them with your arms. (If you have knee problems, grasp your thighs behind your knees instead.)

Hold for 10 seconds.

Slowly extend your legs straight overhead, grasping the backs of your thighs. Flex your toes.

Hold for 10 seconds.

Point your toes and hold for 10 seconds.

Rotate your feet clockwise for 10 seconds.

Rotate your feet counterclockwise for 10 seconds.

Bend your knees and bring your legs slowly in to your chest. Give them a big hug and hold for 10 seconds.

Release.

Benefits: Stretches hamstrings, helps eliminate fatigue in your leg muscles.

FULL BODY STRETCH

Lie on your back on your bed, with your legs extended in front of you and your arms straight overhead.

Stretch from head to toe—try to make yourself taller. Stretch for 10 seconds.

Relax.

Repeat the stretch twice.

Extend your arms and shoulders to your left side, bending sideways from the waist. Keep your legs and hips still. Feel the stretch along your right side.

Hold for 10 seconds.

Release.

Extend your arms and shoulders to your right side and hold for 10 seconds.

Release.

Benefits: Elongates your spine, improves posture, releases tension.

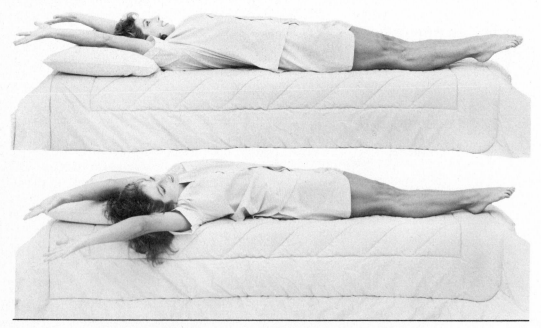

THE HOME STRETCH

Lie on your back on your bed with a pillow under your knees.
Close your eyes.
Inhale deeply through your nose.
Exhale forcefully through your mouth.
Think only of your breathing.
Inhale. Exhale. Inhale. Exhale.
Inhale through your nose for 4 counts.
Exhale through your mouth for 8 counts.
Repeat the sequence 4 times.

Most of us have little sense of the sensation of relaxation. To help gain awareness, produce sensations of tension, then release them slowly. Tense specific muscle groups, then release them. This letting go brings on a restful feeling and helps you fall asleep.

Point your toes for a count of 3. Release them for a count of 3.

Tense your thighs and calves for a count of 3. Release for a count of 3.

Tense your buttocks and hips for a count of 3. Release for a count of 3.

Tense your arms, chest, and shoulders—raise the shoulders, keeping your head on the bed—for a count of 3. Release for a count of 3.

Take a good, deep, slow breath. Exhale. Take another. And another.

Sweet dreams.

GLOSSARY

ABDOMEN the part of the body between the thorax, or upper trunk, and the pelvis; tummy; belly; consists of four pairs of muscles

ACHILLES TENDON the strong tissue formed by the united tendons of the large muscles (gastrocnemius and soleus) running from the back of the calf to the bone of the heel

ADDUCTORS three powerful triangular muscles on the insides of the thighs that—when they contract—bring your legs in toward your body

AEROBIC WORKOUT exercise that uses oxygen as energy and usually lasts more than 20 minutes. It conditions the cardiorespiratory system by causing the heart to pump harder and faster, increasing the amount of blood in your system and the amount of oxygen-carrying hemoglobin in the blood, and by strengthening the muscles that make your lungs expand and contract

BACK EXTENSORS the long vertical muscles that support the back and keep the spinal column in alignment and extension

BICEPS the large flexor muscle at the front of the upper arm, the contraction of which allows you to bend your elbow

BUTTOCKS the two fleshy, rounded protuberances, separated by a median cleft, that form the lower rear part of the trunk and consist largely of the gluteus maximus muscles

CALISTHENICS exercises that emphasize working specific muscle groups against resistance

CARDIOVASCULAR SYSTEM the heart, lungs, and blood vessels

DELTOID the large triangular muscle that covers the shoulder joint and allows you to raise your arm laterally; the anterior deltoids are at the front of the shoulders, the posterior deltoids in the rear

EXTENSOR a muscle that allows you to extend a limb or other body part

FLEXOR a muscle that allows you to bend a limb or other body part

GLUTEUS MAXIMUS the largest buttock muscle

HAMSTRINGS the strong muscles running from the buttocks to the back of the knees

INTERCOSTALS the short muscles located between the ribs at the sides of the waistline that expand and contract your ribs as you breathe

ISOMETRICS exercises that pit one muscle against an immovable object in strong but motionless contraction

ISOTONICS	exercises that permit movement as a muscle or muscles contract
LIGAMENTS	bands of fibrous tissue that connect bones or hold organs in place
LOVE HANDLES	areas of fatty tissue around the hips and back of the waist
MUSCLE	fibrous body tissue that produces movement in the body when contracted
OBLIQUES	thin, flat muscles forming the middle and outer layers of the side walls of the torso
PATELLA	the kneecap
PECTORALS	muscles that connect the walls of the breast or the chest with the bones of the upper arm and the shoulder
QUADRICEPS	the four great extensor muscles in the front of the thighs
RECTUS ABDOMINUS	the long, flat muscle that runs along the front of the torso from the chest bone to the pubic bone
SADDLEBAGS	fatty bulges on the outside of the upper thighs
TENDON	a cord of dense, tough tissue that connects muscle to bone or muscle to muscle

TRAPEZIUS   the large, flat triangular muscles on each side of the upper back

TRICEPS   the muscle on the back of the upper arm, which allows you to straighten your elbow

VERTEBRAE   the segments of bone that make up the spinal column

ABOUT THE AUTHOR AND THE PRODUCER

DENISE AUSTIN is the fitness authority on NBC's "Today" show and a consultant to the President's Council on Physical Fitness and Sports. She stars in several video and audio exercise tapes, including "Rock Hard Tummies," "Rock Aerobics," "Hot Legs," "Total Workout," and "It's Your Body," and she now has her own daily exercise program on ESPN, "Getting Fit with Denise Austin." As a demonstrator-lecturer, Denise has traveled to 45 states and all over the world, including the Soviet Union, and has appeared on hundreds of television programs. She also has been the focus of thousands of newspaper and magazine cover stories and features. She is the national spokesperson for Reebok International Ltd. and for Triangle Health and Fitness Systems. She wants to meet you and let you feel her tummy.

JEROME AGEL has written and/or produced nearly 40 books, including *Take a Deep Breath* (Villard/Random House, 1986). He has collaborated with, among others, Marshall McLuhan, Carl Sagan, Herman Kahn, Stanley Kubrick, Buckminster Fuller, and Isaac Asimov. He is the co-author of two novels and the creator of the computer game "Word of Mouth." Works in progress include *What Happens After You Swallow, 5748 Years of Jewish Humor—But for You 5699, A Press Conference with the U.S. Constitution, The Little Red, White and Blue Book, Pearls of Wisdom,* and two more novels.